Roadworthy
Gearing Up
for the
Race

LeRoy Lawson

STANDARD
PUBLISHING
Cincinnati, Ohio

ISBN 0-7847-7099-9

Edited by Theresa C. Hayes
Cover design by DesignTeam
Inside design by Robert E. Korth

Standard Publishing, Cincinnati, Ohio.
A division of Standex International Corporation.

TABLE OF CONTENTS

THE WAY THROUGH DEEP WATERS

Exodus 14:10-14

When we were children, the drama of Israel's escape from the wicked pharaoh was burned into our imaginations, if not in Sunday school then at the local cinema. A whole generation was enthralled by Cecil B. DeMille's muscular Moses leading his people to the promised land, transmitting the Ten Commandments from God to the Israelites in mesmerizing scenes of smoke and fire.

Our perspective changed as we aged. Now the best part of the story is at the beginning, before Moses hustles his fearful charges across the sea. The Bible presents a dispirited, confused, and often panicky people who have lost faith in God, in their leader, and consequently in themselves. They aren't altogether blameworthy, either. After all, who is this Moses against the might of the pharaoh? And what are these defenseless minions against the armed military? No wonder "they were terrified and cried out to the Lord," scolding Moses for wrenching them away from their security in Egypt.

We look in on the story at the moment the leader and the led confront each other. From the confrontation comes wise counsel, if we are prepared to accept it. You can sometimes learn as much from people's mistakes as from their virtues.

Our question might be, "What do you say to people when the waters are deep and their fears paralyzing?" Moses offers sage counsel. In the first place, he says, "You can't go home again."

Going home is a disillusioning journey.

"They said to Moses, 'Was it because there were no graves in Egypt that you brought us to the desert to die?'"

Their death appears imminent. The heavily armed Egyptians are marching inexorably toward them. The uncrossable sea blocks them. Where can they turn? What can they do?

One thing they can't do: they can't turn back. To return to the pharaoh and cast their lives on his mercy—well, they know (though right now they aren't willing to face up to) the consequences. At the moment, Egypt looks awfully good. If only they had never left.

How often we dream of going home, retreating once more to the starting place, where life was simpler and someone else was responsible and we felt safe. I returned to my hometown recently. It was a good lesson for this romantic, whose reveries often carry me back to my beautiful little county on the Oregon coast. I left there more than 40 years ago. In my dreams, though, it is today as it had been of yore. In my dreams, that is, but not in reality. My sentimental journey was unnerving. The house of my early days is gone now. So is the school of my elementary years. Most of the people I knew then have moved or died. And everything has shrunk.

It's pretty disillusioning, this nostalgic journey backward. Things are almost never as we remember them.

Besides, if there's one truth that's pretty strongly taught in the Scriptures it is this one: God leads forward. Follow Him through the pages of the Bible. You don't find Him at the rear of the lines but in the vanguard, urging His people onward, preparing the way for them. Even at the end, in the book of Revelation, the direction is forward, heavenward, into the future He has prepared for us, with no sighing after what once was but now can be no more.

Like the Israelites, we strain forward not just because that's where God is leading us, but because of what's behind us. In their case, the Egyptians were pressing toward them. To retreat was to face sudden death.

When Henry Ford II was catapulted into the chair of Ford Motor Company as a very young man, company veteran Bunkie Knudsen gave him the advice his own father had given him at the outset of Knudsen's career. "In this business, the competition will bite you if you keep running; if you stand still it will swallow you."[1] I wonder how comforting Ford found this warning. Consoling or not, Ford couldn't deny its accuracy—and not just in the automobile industry. In baseball, for instance, everyone knows "you can't steal second base keeping your foot on first." And as far as Egypt is concerned, if it is freedom you want, you can't go home again!

I'm taking too long on this point because so many people I know are trying to make their way through life looking backward, scared of the future, afraid of success, unable to trust God. Their favorite stratagem is the hasty retreat. Even when that guarantees defeat by the Egyptians.

It's not someone (or everyone) else's fault.

"What have you done to us by bringing us out of Egypt?"

Cowardice and complaining are constant bedfellows. Fear is exposed through faultfinding, finger-pointing. As their leader, Moses is entirely to blame for their predicament. The people are all innocent. If only he had left them alone, everything would have been all right.

Listen carefully to critics. From them you can learn almost nothing about the object of their criticism, but they reveal a great deal about themselves, as in this timeless observation about monks in the sixth century: The ruler of the St. Benedict Monastery lay down the rule that any pilgrim monk from distant parts should be a welcome guest so long as he is content with the hospitality offered him. He can stay as long as he likes. Even if he finds some fault in the place, as long as he "reasonably, and with humility of charity" points it out, the Abbott "shall discuss it prudently, less perchance God has sent him for this very thing."

If, on the other hand, the monk turns out to be a gossip and whiner, not only will he not be invited to become part of the monastery but he will be summarily invited to depart. If he objects to his expulsion? Then "let two stout monks, in the name of God, explain the matter to him." You get the feeling they could be fairly persuasive!

The monastery had learned what we all know. Some people are impossible to satisfy—and whatever is wrong is someone else's fault. They're like the late Randolph Churchill, Sir Winston's journalist son, who was widely known for his irascible personality. When Randolph was hospitalized to have a lung removed, the press announced the trouble wasn't cancer. Writer Evelyn Waugh commented on this "typical triumph of modern science, to find the only part of Randolph that was not malignant and remove it."

We don't enjoy reading of the mewling and grousing of Israel's mob—but we do sympathize. Picturing ourselves in their plight, we wonder whether we would have done otherwise. We have to admit, though, that their fault finding did no good—because it could not—any more than their longing to run back home did.

Tune Up

1. In what ways do you identify with Moses in this passage?

2. In what areas is God nudging you to move forward, but you're stalling a little? (For example, God may be nudging you to do a certain task, face a challenge, or work on a character issue.)

3. What kinds of things make people look backward instead of forward?

4. In what areas of life is it most tempting to make a "hasty retreat"?
   • communicating in relationships
   • problems at work
   • problems at church
   • praying in the midst of troubles
   • planning for the future

How does making a hasty retreat create more trouble than facing the problem?

5. In light of the statement, "Fear is exposed through fault finding, finger-pointing," think of something or someone you're afraid of. Is there anyone or anything you'd like to blame in the midst of your fear? If so, who or what?

It never helps to say, "I told you so."

"Didn't we say to you in Egypt, 'Leave us alone; let us serve the Egyptians?'"

In our remembrances, we're the heroes in our own stories, always the wise counselors in every crisis. With what satisfaction we say, "Didn't I tell you?"

Is it possible the Israelites are remembering a virtue they never had? Or a courage that was never obvious, even when it could have done some good? Have these former slaves, who groaned under their taskmasters' whips, suddenly become proud of the past they once hated?

Their cries recall a well-known remark in Max Planck's *Scientific Autobiography:* "A new scientific truth tends to win acceptance not because its opponents become convinced and declare their conversion, but rather because the opponents gradually die out and the upcoming generation has already become familiar with the truth." Did Planck base his statement only on years of observing scientific controversy —or by also studying the Israelites' 40-year sojourn in the wilderness, a full generation of wandering to give time for the complainers and naysayers and "I-told-you-so-ers" to die out and let a new generation take their place?

Cherish both your freedom and your responsibility.

"It would have been better for us to serve the Egyptians than to die in the desert!" Sounds a little like Buyer's Remorse, doesn't it? Why did I fall for Moses' line? Why did I take the plunge, follow his lead? Why wasn't I content in the misery I knew? Why did I risk everything on something that is turning out to be worse than anything I used to suffer? I liked it better when the Egyptians were in control of my life. If this is freedom, let me out.

Theirs is strikingly like the Cold War slogan of a few decades ago. "Better Red than Dead" shouted the protesters, many of them rebelling against the government's draft of young men to serve in a war they did not understand and would not support. Better to live under a tyrannical pharaoh than die in the sea. Different crisis, same sentiment.

Peter's exhortation is valuable here: "Let none of you suffer . . . as a *busybody* in other men's matters" (1 Peter 4:15, KJV). The full import of the apostle's words lose something in the King James translation, though. The Greek carries a stronger connotation: "Don't steal the other person's leadership. Don't take his oversight responsibilities away from him." The positive could be, as our grandmothers used to tell us, "Tend to your own knitting."

But responsibility is not the favorite topic of today's masses any more than of the crowd crying to Moses. There must have been a time, back in Egypt, when their backs were aching and their feet were sore, when they longed to be free, yearned to throw off the yoke of their hated masters. But that day is forgotten now. Freedom? Yes. The responsibility that goes with it? No.

Casey Stengel, the legendary baseball manager of the New York Yankees, said he knew the secret of success. It is "to keep the five guys who hate you away from the five guys who haven't made up their minds." At this moment, the balance was swinging against Moses; the Egyptians already hated him, the Israelites were quickly coming around to their

point of view. For that matter, Moses himself must have
been feeling pretty put upon. Reading through the accounts
of his struggles to lead this intractable nation, rebelling and
resisting and complaining the whole way to the promised
land, I recall an old not-so-funny joke I heard years ago
about a couple of guys riding a tandem bicycle up a steep
hill. The front man nearly collapsed in exhaustion at the top,
while his partner on the back seat hadn't even broken into a
sweat. "Wow, that was a wild ride," the back-seat driver said,
"but you didn't have to worry. I had my foot on the brake the
entire time, so thanks to me we didn't slip back!"

Responsibility!

════════ Tune Up ════════

1. If you had been one of the whining Israelites, which of
   these complaints would you have been most likely to
   have made? (Let a spouse or friend help you with this!)

   • All this misery is Moses' fault. (Blaming)
   • We tried to tell Moses to leave us alone, but he
     wouldn't listen! (Saying I told you so)
   • I want to go home. (Looking backward instead of
     forward)

2. When people blame, say "I told you so," or look backward, what do they need to realize?

3. In what ways could you take responsibility for the goals or tasks that scare you?

Act brave, even when you're scared.

"Moses answered the people, 'Do not be afraid. Stand firm and you will see the deliverance the Lord will bring you today. The Egyptians you see today you will never see again.'"

Note the order of the promise: first they must overpower their fears and stand firm. Then they will see deliverance. It's a constant biblical refrain, this call to bravery in the face of overwhelming odds. What alternative do they have? Panic, of course. And flight. Moses is summoning them to a bravery they don't feel in the face of an enemy they can't defeat by themselves. They must do what they *can* do— which is to stand. Then they must trust Moses and the Lord—Moses, hoping that he's telling the truth, and the Lord, hoping He'll come through as Moses insists He will.

From our American civil rights movement has come a story of similar bravery, a courage once again born of very limited choices: Rosa Parks almost single-handedly sparked the movement in Montgomery, Alabama, when she refused to move to the back of the bus. She is often quoted as saying she sat in the white people's section because she was too tired to move to the back. That wasn't what happened, she says. "People always say that I didn't give up my seat because I was tired, but that isn't true. I was not tired physically, or no more tired than I usually was at the end of a working day. I was not old, although some people have an image of me as being old then. I was 42. No, the only tired I was, was tired of giving in."[2]

The alternative to giving in was not giving in.

For the Israelites, the alternative to being afraid was standing firm.

My wife Joy and I stayed in the Holiday Inn when we attended the 1998 North American Christian Convention in St. Louis. The city, like most large American metropolises, has been battling an unenviable crime rate. The hotel feels compelled to warn its guests to take extra precautions during their stay. In our room we found this letter:

> Dear Guest: To assist you in having an enjoyable stay at the Holiday Inn Convention Center, we urge you to take the same care for your security and safety as you would at home. The local police and every employee at this hotel are on the alert to deter and prevent any crime. We enlist your assistance in this effort too. [Here follow many suggestions for safety. I am listing the pertinent ones.]
>
> - Do not leave your valuables visibly exposed in your vehicle (this includes radar detectors and mobile telephones). Remember to lock your vehicle when leaving it.
> - When in your hotel room, keep your door double locked (turn the dead bolt).
> - Use the chain provided on the door.
> - Never sit in your room with the guest room door left open.
> - Ensure that connecting room doors are secured properly.
> - Never invite strangers to your room.
> - Before opening your door when someone knocks, identify the person by looking through the peephole. If you are concerned, call the hotel operator. Do not open the door to a stranger without positively verifying the reason for the visit.
> - Be observant! Look around before venturing into large parking lots and/or unfamiliar areas of this city.
> - When anything appears suspicious or someone appears to be loitering on the property, contact management immediately.

These suggestions are not meant to alarm you, however crime can occur anywhere, anytime. We do not want your stay spoiled by such an encounter. These tips merely express our desire to make your hotel visit safe and successful.

How's that for making you feel at home? I have some friends who solve the problem by never venturing into a city. Their fear immobilizes them. Read the letter again and you'll notice a similarity to the first part of Moses' charge: Do not be afraid. Stand firm.

What the Holiday Inn leaves out is the part of the equation that makes it possible to be calm in the face of danger—the belief that "the Lord will bring deliverance today."

The Greek philosopher Epictetus, whose relationship with God was far from what Moses enjoyed, could nevertheless assert, "For it is not death or hardship that is a fearful thing, but fear of death and hardship." Shakespeare put it a little more familiarly, "Cowards die many times before their deaths; the valiant never taste of death but once." Moses says it best: "Do not be afraid. Stand firm and you will see the deliverance the Lord will bring you today."

Trust God

"The Lord will fight for you; you need only to be still."

Upon this truth Moses rests his case: You can count on God. Your physical strength, your assembled arms, your cunning or strategizing are useless to you now. Be still. Trust God.

Antoine de Saint-Exupery makes a case for bravery without reference to God. He says that "once men are caught up in an event they cease to be afraid. Only the unknown frightens men. But once a man has faced the unknown, that terror becomes known."[3] Would that he were right. But he isn't. The Israelites weren't facing an unknown. They knew very well what they were confronting: certain destruction at the hands of their former taskmasters. They knew the Egyptians, they knew the depths of the sea, they knew the odds against their surviving. What they also knew, but needed to have Moses remind them, was that God was with them. They could trust Him.

The dictionary yields an interesting definition of trust: "the assured reliance on another's integrity." Moses was asking the people to believe in God's integrity, to accept that He would do what He has promised.

They could, if they would, look to the promise and not the Egyptians.

I heard of a speaker at a Rotary club who responded to a question about the current economic recession. She tacked a big sheet of white paper on the wall, then made a black spot on it with her pencil. She asked a man in the front row what he saw. "A black spot," he said. Next she asked nearly every person in the room. The answer was unanimous. Then she launched into her lecture. "Yes, there is a little black spot, but none of you mentioned the big sheet of white paper. And that's my speech."

Yes, the Egyptians are coming. They are the spot. But you haven't noticed God.

A little Bible study might be helpful here. Do you recognize any of the following verses? What do you make of them?

> I know whom I have believed, and am persuaded that he is able to keep that which I have committed unto him against that day.
>
> 2 Timothy 1:12 (KJV)

> When I am afraid, I will trust in you. In God, whose word I praise, in God I trust; I will not be afraid. What can mortal man do to me?
>
> Psalm 56:3, 4

> So do not fear, for I am with you; do not be dismayed, for I am your God. I will strengthen you and help you; I will uphold you with my righteous right hand.
>
> Isaiah 41:10

So we say with confidence, "The Lord is my helper; I will not be afraid. What can man do to me?"

Hebrews 13:6

Do not be anxious about anything, but in everything, by prayer and petition, with thanksgiving, present your requests to God. And the peace of God, which transcends all understanding, will guard your hearts and your minds in Christ Jesus.

Philippians 4:6, 7

You know the rest of the story. God delivered the Israelites, they marched through the Red Sea, the Egyptians were drowned, and Moses' leadership was vindicated.

I'm more concerned about the rest of our stories, yours and mine. That we will face deep waters is inevitable. That we will sometimes seemed trapped between the enemy behind and an uncrossable sea before is equally predictable.

But that we have only two choices—to surrender to the enemy or be drowned in the deep waters—that simply is not true. We have a third option. We can trust God to lead us to safety.

Hasn't He so far?

Won't He again?

Tune Up

1. What are some words that describe what goes on inside you when you're "tired of giving in" as Rosa Parks was?

2. Imagine that God were to appear to you today. How might God personalize Exodus 14:13? ("Do not be afraid. Stand firm and you will see the deliverance the Lord will bring you today.")

Do not be afraid, _____ *(your name)*. Stand firm and you will see . . . *(finish this)*.

3. In light of the verse, "The Lord will fight for you; you need only to be still," what are some ways in which you need to "be still" when you don't want to be?

4. Think of a situation in your life in which there seems to be (as it seemed to the Israelites) only two options: surrender to the enemy or be drowned in the deep waters.

The third option is to trust God to lead you to safety. What does that look like, compared to the other two options?

[1]Peter Collier and David Horowitz, *The Fords.* New York, et al: Summit Books, 1987.

[2]Parker J. Palmer, *The Courage to Teach: Exploring the Landscape of a Teacher's Life.* San Francisco: Jossey-Bass Publishers, 1998.

[3]Antoine de Saint-Exupery, *Wind, Sand and Stars.* New York: Tim Reading Program, 1939, 1940.

CHAPTER 2

THE WAY THROUGH FEAR
1 Samuel 17:1-51; Psalm 23:4

Every neighborhood has its bully, I suppose. We probably had several in my hometown, but the one I've remembered for a lifetime was Charlie, a really big, really mean kid my age. Six. We were in the same first grade class. I don't recall having any trouble at school, but I do recollect being terrorized by this brute several times as I was walking to or from home. I held the class record in one category. Size. Minimum. As I said, Charlie was big, really big, for a first grader. And he was an exhibitionist. He loved showing off his strength. He was pretty circumspect, though, in picking his opponents. I think I was the only one. I was what you might call a sure thing.

One day something snapped. I decided I wasn't going to take his brutalizing any longer. "Decided" may be the wrong word. I can't imagine that I weighed the pros and cons and then reasoned my way to a rational conclusion. It was, you might say, pure adrenaline. I just got mad. I was six years old and I was not going to go through life being picked on. I had seen the Charles Atlas ads that were popular then, and I didn't like how much that puny weakling in them looked like an older version of me. So when Charlie ambushed me that afternoon, I didn't back away or turn and run. With an excess of hormonal bravery surging through my veins I counter-pounced, knocking him down (he collapsed more from surprise than fright, I suspect), somehow pinned and held him—and made him promise never to do that to me again. I was fierce. He seemed to believe I meant it. He promised to leave me alone, not enthusiastically but with some sincerity. Then he got up, hit me, and ran away faster than I could catch him—and you can bet I tried. That was our last encounter.

You can understand, can't you, why I love to revisit the story of David and Goliath? It's particularly gratifying when the little guy wins. Right over might. Quality over quantity.

By the way, my Charlie story is the only one I have like it. Ordinarily I was much more like Harry Truman as a boy. When the former president was in his eighties, he enjoyed appearing at the Truman Library in Independence, Missouri, to chat with the visitors and show them around the place. It was during a talking tour for students and other visitors that he stopped in the auditorium for a question and answer time. A small boy asked, "Mr. President, was you popular when you was a boy?"

"Why, no," the president answered. "I was never popular. The popular boys were the ones who were good at games and had big, tight fists. I was never like that. Without my glasses I was blind as a bat, and to tell the truth, I was kind of a sissy. If there was any danger of getting into a fight, I always ran."[1]

Was Mr. Truman being modest to encourage his young interrogator, or was he really a sissy? From everything else we know of the feisty senior statesman, it's hard to believe his self-description. Prudent, perhaps, but not a sissy. Well, there's at least one difference between the young Harry and David. Jesse's son didn't run. And his bully wasn't a Charlie, but a Goliath of a man.

Goliath. As a child, I pictured him as humongous, gargantuan, larger-than-life—towering much higher than the biblical "nine feet tall." In my imagination he was more like one hundred feet from sole to crown. But on one point the Bible and I agreed: he was one bad dude! Bad, at least, in the eyes of the Israelites. And boastful. His boasting convinced Saul's army. They weren't at all eager to take him on.

His bragging wasn't without reason, of course. Nor did anybody think less of him for his lack of humility. In the literature of most ancient peoples, boasting is considered a virtue—if the braggart could produce, that is. And Goliath had already proved himself virtuous.

It's not a bad ploy, this calculated crowing. American hammer-thrower Harold Connolly seemed to be doing some of it himself during the 1956 Melbourne Summer Olympics. In his practice session, Connolly carried his ball and chain ten to fifteen feet beyond where he had been able to cast his longest throws. There in the soft turf he pounded impressions like those a hammer makes when it thuds into the ground. He marked one with an American flag. When Russian throwers arrived for their afternoon practice session, they were astounded their opponent could throw so far. Trying to match his supposed feat, they threw with all their might. As a result they wore themselves out practicing and affected their carefully practiced technique. Connolly walked away with the gold medal. His "bragging" paid off.[2]

Goliath isn't merely boasting, either. There's a certain economy in his dare, a consideration for the troops in both camps. By his proposal, only one person would need to die instead of the hundreds who could fall in pitched battle. One could almost say there's something honorable about his challenge, especially when you look at how things worked out. Once Goliath was knocked out of the contest, the Israelites took advantage of their superior numbers and slaughtered the Philistines. What are we to make of their unsportsmanlike conduct?

When you read the account from the Philistine point of view, you can't be really critical of Goliath. He's their Michael Jordan, predictably leading his teammates to championships. (Do you think the world-famous Chicago Bulls resented Jordan, even though he was getting most of the glory? He is their hero.) But we read the story from the point

of view of Saul's army, and to them, Goliath is the enemy—
spelled large!

<hr>

Tune Up

1. In what situations do you feel like the "little guy"—
   maybe you're "smaller" in skills, wealth, reputation,
   intellect, verbal ability?

2. Apparently David was not bothered by Goliath's
   "calculated crowing," but if you had been David, how
   might Goliath's "calculated crowing" have affected
   you?

   ❏ Bring out the best in you
   ❏ Annoy you to the point of distraction
   ❏ Intimidate you—then weaken you

   ❏ Other: _____

<hr>

I wonder how popular this episode is with women. It is a
man's story. It smells of the locker room, captures the drama
of the battlefield. There is no softening female presence.
"Choose a *man* and have him come down to me," Goliath
roars. No one doubts what he means. Send me a fighter, a
brave soldier, somebody skilled in the martial arts—someone
worthy of me. This is machismo talk. Later, when David

steps forward, Goliath is incensed. "He looked David over and saw that he was only a boy, ruddy and handsome, and he *despised him.*" He demanded a man and they sent him a boy. Insulting.

Yet in one sense David measures up to Goliath's machismo. He is not afraid. As for the rest of Saul's army, "on hearing the Philistine's words, Saul and all the Israelites were dismayed and terrified." Even the king trembles before the giant.

Their trepidation reminds me of the story former Commissioner of the Royal Canadian Mounted Police Norman Inkster told. It features a police exam and some would-be constables. They were given a hypothetical situation to test their intelligence, judgment, and leadership skills. Here's the scenario: You arrive at a gas explosion to find several casualties. There is a drunk driver, whom you recognize as the wife of a senior official. Nearby a woman starts to give birth. Not much farther away someone is drowning in a canal while at the same time a fierce fight breaks out threatening severe damage or even loss of life. In a few words describe what you would do.

One applicant wrote, "I would remove my uniform and mingle with the crowd."[3]

I admire his judgment.

Goliath would not have. I suspect he would be more inclined to applaud my high school history teacher cum football coach. He was an excellent instructor. I can't speak firsthand of his coaching ability. I limited my football participation to yelling from the grandstand. I have never forgotten the day he addressed all us fellows in an assembly and informed us that if we didn't play football we weren't men, we were pansies. That was one of my nicknames for a long time afterward. The coach was just not impressed with my prowess on the piano. He belonged to the Goliath school of thought. (If Goliath disdained the young David's manhood, I don't even want to contemplate what he would have thought of mine.)

Yet courage takes different forms, doesn't it? As Jonathan Swift acutely observed, "He was a bold man who first ate an oyster." My coach, no longer the young athlete he was in my high school days, would undoubtedly define manhood today with a little less emphasis on the machismo and considerably more on wisdom, responsibility, self-sacrifice, and inner strength—qualities we associate more with the spiritual dimension of being. Such characteristics do not make for exciting football games and may not be the basics of military boot camp, but they do even the odds when a David takes on Goliath.

This face-off in the Valley of Elah is not to be just a contest between two duelists, however. Cultures are clashing, ethnic histories colliding here as these traditional enemies, Philistines and Israelites, gear up to do battle. The Bible presents the encounter as the pitting of God's people versus the Philistines. These words have, to students of English literature, a familiar ring. The Victorian poet and essayist Matthew Arnold borrowed the biblical term as a epithet for crass, commercial, money-grubbing types. This is not exactly fair to the Philistines, who lived centuries before industrial materialism captured Western civilization, but in the term today you catch a whiff of the good guys sweating it out against the bad guys in 1 Samuel 17.

What the modern reader finds ironic is that Saul, the Israelite king himself, can be charged and found guilty of being a "Philistine" by today's definition. Money dominates his thinking:

The king will give great wealth to the man who kills him.
He will also give him his daughter in marriage
and will exempt his father's family from taxes in Israel.

The best Saul can offer his champion is property—money, material goods, exemption from taxes—and his daughter. Property. (Our traditional wedding ceremony descends from the day, not so long ago, when daughters were evaluated as Saul values his: "Who gives [because she is yours to give, because she is not an independent soul, because she belongs to you and can at your word be transferred to the ownership of another] this woman to be married to this man?" Fortunately, these old words have taken on a more symbolic and less literal meaning. But King Saul isn't speaking poetically. He offers his property.)

More than property is at stake, though. This is power talking. An oriental potentate, Saul cannot be overruled in his realm. Like one of today's middle eastern monarchs (Saddam Hussein comes to mind), when Saul speaks there is no opposition. His is a common misunderstanding of leadership, the wish-fulfillment of the child who says, "When I get big I'm going to get my own way." So politicians and corporation CEOs and little tyrants of all kinds become despots of their realm. For a while. Until somebody stronger rises to overthrow them. A Goliath, perhaps. Or a David.

We pause at this point in the story. Having been in some leadership role for most of my life, I marvel at the vast distance between people's fantasies of a democratic leader's power and the little authority he can exercise. An occasional critic will scold me because, as pastor or president or chairman I do not take immediate action to correct this or that inequity or stamp out a certain problem or summarily dismiss an offending subordinate. From the tone and the peremptory demands of his letter it is apparent that I am expected, like King Saul, merely to utter the word and my critic's will will be done. Wrong. Leadership, at least in a democracy (and for that matter, in most monarchies) does not enjoy absolute control. Not dictating but persuading, modeling, cajoling, entreating, and even haranguing are required. What do you suppose would go through the mind of a modem American president if he were to read this passage?

Place the president in Saul's role for the moment. He wants to motivate his young champion to risk his life against the giant. The president could, if he wanted, give the aspiring hero money from his personal estate but he would never presume that he could promise huge sums from the United States Treasury without consultation. And as for promising his daughter's hand in marriage without her consent—well, who could imagine? And what would Congress have to say about his exempting not only the contestant but his father's family from taxes? The best the president could offer would be a promise to work with the Budget Director, attempt to persuade his daughter to consider the young man as a possible husband, and to set his Congressional liaison officer to work rounding up the votes to get a special law passed on behalf of the young hero and his family—for a generation or two.

What a different world is ours from David's! While we can justly draw many parallels in this encounter between then and now, these verses remind us that we have left American democracy for the alien machinations of absolutist monarchy.

Speaking of alien—David finds himself in a pretty strange place, too. He has never before been in this kind of combat. Until now, his main sparring partners have been lions and bears. "But David said to Saul, 'Your servant has been keeping his father's sheep. When a lion or a bear came and carried off a sheep from the flock, I went after it, struck it and rescued the sheep from its mouth. When it turned on me, I seized it by its hair, struck it and killed it. Your servant has killed both the lion and the bear; this uncircumcised Philistine will be like one of them, because he has defied the armies of the living God.'"

These are pretty unusual credentials for convincing the king that David is his man, but they don't seem strange at all to David. As far as he is concerned, the skills acquired protecting his flock from four-legged predators readily transfer to protecting Saul's army from two-legged ones. Bear- and lion-slaying tactics will work just fine.

Tune Up

1. What different forms of courage have you witnessed?
(For example, courage with words, courage with quiet
actions, courage with daring actions, courage to do
nothing.)

2. Saul offered material wealth to motivate someone to be
courageous. In your experience, what do you think
motivates people to be courageous?

3. Dr. Lawson comments on the relative lack of power
that a pastor, president, or chairman has in an unjust
situation. If that's true, what is a Christian to do in an
unjust situation?

4. God apparently prepared David to meet Goliath through David's encounters with lions and bears. How has God prepared you for a situation in your life that requires courage?

The David/Goliath encounter invites meditation on what God requires of His warriors, especially since the men and women God calls into His service so often seem far from equal to their tasks. The great saints through the ages have confessed their inadequacies. Who among the biblical heroes can you name who felt "worthy" of God's call? If there is any dominant theme coursing through the pages of the Bible, it is that God chooses the least likely, the smallest, the weakest, the apparently most unfit to do his work, "lest any man should boast."

The great nineteenth-century African missionary David Livingstone comes to mind. His humble beginning illustrates that of so many of God's faithful. One Sunday the minister of Stanford Rivers fell sick after the morning service and young Livingstone was summoned to preach for the evening meeting. When the time came David stood before the assembly, read his text very deliberately, looked up at the people—and froze. His sermon was gone. He couldn't remember a word of it. Finally, in desperation, he said, "Friends, I have forgotten all I had to say." With that he abruptly left the chapel. Not an auspicious beginning for a would-be missionary. He wrote later from Elizabethtown in Africa, "I am a very poor preacher, having a bad delivery." He said of those who had to listen to him, "Some of them said that if they knew I had to preach again they would not enter the chapel."[4]

You know the rest of the story. The famed Dr. Livingstone never did make his mark as a preacher, but it was not to preach that he was called. When he aligned himself with God's purposes for his life, his courage grew with its increasing competence until he was ready to take on a continent in God's name.

In the present story, it is not so much that the hero feels inadequate but that everyone else considers him so. I mentioned that Goliath despises David. That's not the worst of it for the young shepherd. Not only the prophet, as Jesus said, but sometimes a future king is without honor among his own: "When Eliab, David's oldest brother, heard him speaking with the men, he burned with anger at him and asked, 'Why have you come down here? And with whom did you leave those few sheep in the desert? I know how conceited you are and how wicked your heart is; you came down only to watch the battle.'" Why is Eliab so angry? Is it protectiveness speaking? Sibling rivalry? Big brothers don't always shine in scriptural stories. We are led to believe that the bossy Eliab has been pretty hard on David before: "'Now what have I done?' said David. 'Can't I even speak?'"

His brother Eliab, the other men to whom he turned, the king himself—they all doubted. As the king said, "You are not able to go out against this Philistine and fight him; you are only a boy." And Goliath sneered. Yet they could not quench David's ardor. How did he get this strong sense of self, or should I call it more accurately this unwavering reliance on God, the quiet assurance that he is right even though everyone else doubts? Whatever you call it, and wherever it comes from, it's the stuff leaders are made of, isn't it?

We recall that unlikely parliamentary genius Winston Churchill, who gives us a secular parallel to David's experience. When Neville Chamberlain returned to London after yielding to all of Hitler's demands in September 1938, he declared he had achieved "peace in our time." The crowds cheered. Chamberlain was welcomed in the House of Commons as a hero. But he was no hero to Churchill, who stood before five hundred MPs to announce that in Chamberlain's deal England had "sustained a tragic and unmitigated defeat."

In time, England turned to the lonely dissenter to defend them against Hitler. Call it whatever you will, this ability to stand alone against the jeers of the opposition is essential to leadership.

David has it. He will not be run off by Goliath's ridiculing or his family's patronizing. He will fight—and he will fight in his own way. "David fastened on his [the king's] sword over the tunic and tried walking around, because he was not used to them. 'I cannot go in these,' he said to Saul, 'because I am not used to them.' So he took them off."

Tune Up

1. Can you think of examples from Scripture, or from life today where God chose the least likely, the smallest, the weakest, the apparently unfit to do His work? If so, name those people.

2. Why is it difficult to be courageous when your friends and relatives are doubting you (as David's did)?

3. What do you think are the ingredients in a "strong sense of self" which David had? When have you (like David) used weapons that were different from weapons others used? (For example, silence instead of talking, waiting instead of moving ahead, kindness instead of evil.)

Against the fully-armed Goliath, David looks pitifully vulnerable. He has his sling and five stones. Period. Goliath towers before him with his "bronze helmet on his head . . . a coat of scale armor of bronze weighing five thousand shekels; on his legs he wore bronze greaves, and a bronze javelin was slung on his back. His spear shaft was like a weaver's rod, and its iron point weighed six hundred shekels. His shield bearer went ahead of him." It looks like no contest. But David has something else: "I come against you in the name of the Lord Almighty, the God of the armies of Israel, whom you have defied. This day the Lord will hand you over to me. . . ." End of contest.

What a sight, the giant and the boy, racing toward the decision. A more unevenly matched pair you can't imagine. It has something of the comic element in it, like Russia's diminutive Nikita Khrushchev ordering one of his subordinates, "Comrade General, please stand back a bit so I can look you in the eye."[5]

David looks Goliath in the eye, measures the distance between them, hoists and whirls his slingshot and stone—and in an instant the battle is over. One shot, hurled with precise accuracy, is enough. The boy, son of Jesse of Bethlehem, is on the rise.

We hasten to the moral of the story. What are mere swords and spears and javelins against the Lord's anointed?

A footnote on the moral: David's reliance on the Lord is a far cry from the passive "Let go and let God" mantra so often used to excuse our doing nothing. As far as David is concerned, the battle is never himself against Goliath. Nor is it God against Goliath. David and God are in the battle together, each doing his assigned part. David trusts God to deliver—as God trusts David to be courageous—so that in the end "the whole world will know that there is a God in Israel" and that "it is not by sword or spear that the Lord saves, for the battle is the Lord's, and he will give all of you into our hands."

David has played his role magnificently. Courage and trust were required of him; he could already offer a disciplined physique and practiced skills. He was physically and spiritually fit for the trial. Having done all he could do, David had but to rely on God for the rest.

From this experience and many others like them, David would one day write,

> Even though I walk
> through the valley of the shadow of death,
> I will fear no evil,
> for you are with me.
>
> Psalm 23:4

and

> Cast your cares on the Lord and he will sustain you;
> he will never let the righteous fall.
>
> Psalm 55:22

That's a promise.

Tune Up

1. David had to trust God to deliver while God trusted David to be courageous. Which is more difficult for you at this time—trust or courage?

2. In what ways has God reassured you lately to be more trusting or more courageous?

3. David was physically and spiritually fit for his trial. Having done all he could do, he had but to rely on God for the rest. Are you prepared for whatever God may send your way? Have you done all that you can do to be ready for service?

[1]Bert Cochran, *Harry Truman and the Crisis Presidency.* New York: Funk & Wagnalls, 1973.

[2]C. R. Creekmore, "Games Athletes Play," *Psychology Today,* July 1984.

[3]E. Ray Jones, "Minister Muses," *Clearwater Christian,* June 21, 1995.

[4]George Seaver, *David Livingstone: His Life and Letters.* New York: Harper, 1965.

[5]Edward Crankshaw, *Khrushchev Remembers.* Boston, Toronto: Little, Brown and Company, 1970.

CHAPTER 3

THE WAY THROUGH DOUBT

2 Kings 5:1-14

I don't remember the author now, but I still feel the sting of embarrassment. I was reading a book on preaching—a pretty good one as I recall. Otherwise the slap wouldn't have hurt so much. The writer took a swipe at preachers whose sermon titles are just too cute. The specific example he cited was one very close to the title of my first sermon, which I called, cutely, "Seven Ducks in Muddy Water." It was about Naaman, commander of the army of the king of Aram (or Syria), whom the prophet Elisha cured of his leprosy by prescribing that Naaman go and wash himself seven times in the Jordan River (those dips are the seven ducks—get it?) and he would be healed.

You need to grant me a little grace. I was just a sophomore in high school. It wasn't even an original title. My mentor borrowed it from a well-known preacher; she thought the passage would be one that a novice could handle and if the congregation remembered nothing else, they could remember the title!

Well, that was long ago and far away, and though I still blush a little as I recall both the title and the content of that first sermon, my mentor was right. It was an excellent text for a beginning preacher. What better theme could an initiate into the homiletic arts consider than this one on the trust that leads to healing?

Trust and obedience

Naaman symbolizes any high-octane achiever. His is a record to be proud of. He is highly regarded by peers and subordinates alike; even his king respects him. He gained his reputation the hard way: he earned it, although the biblical writer (is he smiling as he writes it?) says that actually "*the Lord* had given victory to Aram." Naaman just led the troops. But then the general is neither the first nor the last person to get the credit for something God has done.

Naaman's reputation is deserved, though, and his king has every reason to rely on him. "He was a valiant soldier."

A valiant fighter, but a flawed human being. "He had leprosy." Unfortunately, the term does not tell us exactly what afflicted Naaman. The Bible attaches leprosy to a variety of symptoms, some of which modern medicine gives other labels.

There are several types of leprosy. Biblical leprosy is most likely a severe type of psoriasis, a form of the disease relatively rare in modern times. In Israel, lepers were quarantined, forced to wear mourning clothes and to drive people safely away by their plaintive cries, "Unclean! Unclean!" Fortunately for Naaman, these extreme measures were not the custom in Syria. The general was pitied but not shunned. However, his reluctant willingness to seek the prophet in Israel, to say nothing of his readiness to follow the advice of a mere servant girl, shows how worrisome his condition was. If it progressively worsened, as leprosy was wont to do, his career could be jeopardized.

The Syrian's affliction reminds us that many famous leaders have served in spite of severe disabilities. Franklin Delano Roosevelt comes immediately to mind, guiding his gaunt and frightened nation through the deprivations of the Great Depression and then the horrors of a world war—from a wheelchair. His biographers unanimously credit his crippling polio with converting the spoiled rich kid into the dynamic leader Roosevelt became.

The list of achievers and the disability they succeeded "in spite of" is long: Einstein's dyslexia, Beethoven's deafness, Grant's alcoholism, Calvin's multiple illnesses, Lincoln's depressions, Helen Keller's blindness and deafness, Theodore Roosevelt's asthma, and so on. Think of your own circle of acquaintances. Whom among them has accomplished much without the advantage of a serious disability? For that matter, whom can you name who has everything, including perfect health, who has achieved much? When does a challenge become a handicap—and when is it instead a stimulus to attainment? And what makes the difference? Whatever your answer, you'll have to admit Naaman is in pretty impressive company.

Tune Up

1. Why do you think Scripture is full of "high-octane achievers" with distinct flaws? (Paul's thorn in the flesh; Moses' early murder of an Egyptian; Noah's drunkenness; Samuel's failed children; Jacob's manipulating ways; Matthew's questionable occupation of tax collecting.)

2. How do flaws (and past mistakes) make us more likely to let God use us?

3. What, if any, flaws have actually helped you in the long run—motivating you, giving you determination? (If not you, then perhaps someone you know.)

Naaman might be a little impatient with my musing. He isn't speculating on the contribution of his handicap to his development. He just wants to be healed, wants healing bad enough he finally makes the trek to see Elisha.

But then he can't believe his ears. The Jordan? He has to dip himself in the Jordan River? "Are not Abana and Pharpar, the rivers of Damascus, better than any of the waters of Israel? Couldn't I wash in them and be cleansed?"

He could, of course, if the critical ingredient in Elisha's prescription is the water. As rivers go, the Jordan is not much to brag about when you measure it against the world's biggest and best. Naaman has taken its measure. It is nothing compared with the waters of his homeland. But to his chauvinistic thinking, nothing else in Israel can equal Syria's splendors, either.

Water, though, isn't the issue. So far, Naaman's is a pretty mechanical perspective. He hasn't caught on to the real source of healing that Elisha offers; he is looking for some-*thing* he can take, some*one* who can touch his body and miraculously cure it. If water is the agent, then the healing must be in the water, or at least in the washing—and for that, surely, Syrian waters are to be preferred.

It's difficult for a preacher not to draw a parallel between Naaman's opinion and that of some latter day baptismal candidates who think that simply dipping themselves in a baptismal pool will save them. They believe the magic is in the water. One such lady approached me for baptism several years ago. When I discovered that she wanted nothing to do with a church and had no intention of doing anything further to follow Jesus, I had to decline her request. I talked to her about what baptism entails, how it pictures our joining the body of Christ, and how it is all wrapped up with repentance and faith and obedience. She would hear none of it. The ultimate life insurance was what she wanted, and being immersed "for the remission of sins" sounded good, but she had no interest in baptism as the inauguration of a new life of trust and obedience. I couldn't accommodate her. So, like Naaman, she "turned and went off in a rage."

Naaman's story would end here if the cooler heads of his servants did not prevail. "My father," they implore, "if the prophet had told you to do some great thing, would you not have done it? How much more, then, when he tells you, 'Wash and be cleansed'!"

Like observant servants everywhere, they know their master's weakness. A great man does "the great things," at least in his own eyes. His reward is in the chase, his joy in the challenge, his sense of superiority in mastering what lesser mortals fear to try. One doesn't make general by tackling the little things that anybody else can do. But in spiritual matters, in contrast to military ones, it is often through seemingly inconsequential (but nonetheless difficult) events that major breakthroughs occur. Something as minor, for example, as a dip in a river—and as difficult as obeying the orders of a nobody like this Israelite prophet Elisha. As hard as a general taking orders from a civilian. Something like that.

Tune Up

1. If you were to ask God for a healing, what would it be? (For example, healing of finances, health, relationships.)

2. When has God used something (or someone) that was supposedly beneath you to help you as He used the relatively puny Jordan River in Naaman's life?

3. In God's use of that obscure object or person, what was your doubt based on?

4. Although Naaman was unwilling to dip himself into the lowly Jordan River, he was willing to listen to "lowly" people—his servants. Why do you think he did that?

"Trust and Obey" is a hymn well known to Christians of my generation. Its repetitious chorus is permanently etched in our memories:

"Trust and obey, for there's no other way
To be happy in Jesus, but to trust and obey."

Simple, even simplistic, but for the Christian, true. And for Naaman, there is no way around it, even for a great general. If there is to be healing, he has to trust and obey.

President Ronald Reagan, preparing to meet Russia's Mikhail Gorbachev in Geneva, gave a new twist to trusting and obeying. "Since the dawn of the nuclear age," he observed, "every American president has sought to limit and end the dangerous competition in nuclear arms. I have no higher priority than to finally realize that dream." He had convinced himself that Gorbachev was someone he could do business with. He was ready to risk America's future on an agreement between the two super-powers. But he also said he would live by an old Russian adage: *"Dovorey no provorey.* Trust, but verify."[1]

Trusting Mr. Gorbachev probably did not come easy to Ronald Reagan, whose career was built on fighting Communism. Yet world peace was at stake. So was his legacy, of which he was becoming acutely conscious in the final years of his presidency. He dared to hope he could realize through person-to-person diplomacy what earlier presidents and his own aides had failed to achieve. He dreamed of ending the dangerous competition in nuclear arms. The reward was worth the risk. So he would trust tentatively, all the while looking for reasons to justify the trust.

That's all the servants ask of Naaman. Trust the prophet tentatively, if you must, and verify, certainly, at least to the point of testing the prescription in the Jordan. But trust. Try it. Go to the river. Obey the order. See what happens.

Trust and humility

Proverbs 3:5 offers sound advice: "Trust in the Lord with all thine heart; and lean not unto thine own understanding" (KJV). What believer would quarrel with this maxim? But what if the Lord chooses to speak through the hired help? Or makes his spokesman an eccentric, discourteous, even insulting, prophet? What's a person to do?

Naaman finally makes up his mind to trust. He takes his servants' advice. He performs, however reluctantly, the ablutions the prophet demands. "So he went down and dipped himself in the Jordan seven times, as the man of God had told him, and his flesh was restored and became clean like that of a young boy."

First the humility, then the healing.

Humility is the attitude, submission the act. Someone has said, "Tell a man there are 300 billion stars in the universe and he'll believe you. Tell him a bench has wet paint on it and he'll have to touch it to be sure." It isn't humility that enables him to swallow a scientist's astronomical claims. It's helplessness. He has no way of verifying. He readily yields to the expert. But wet paint? Now that's something he knows about. He doesn't need to take a professional's word for it. His judgment's as good as anybody else's. He knows wet paint when he sees (or at least touches) it.

This same fellow is also pretty good at telling you who's going to Heaven and who isn't. He doesn't need any expert on this subject, either, even though the touch test can't be applied. What gives him confidence is the solemn conviction that nobody, even the most learned theologian, knows more about Heaven than he does. According to a *Time* poll, for example, most Americans are confident that Heaven is their destination. This is something they know! But alas, they do not expect to see many of their neighbors there. Just 18 percent said they thought all their friends would join them in Heaven. About spiritual things, and about their own spiritual excellence, you see, they are the authorities. (An illuminating sidelight from that same poll: 87 percent believe they are going to Heaven, but only 67 percent believe it exists. These figures present, it would seem, some challenges.)

To men and women who consider their eternal future with such aplomb, Oswald Chambers offers sound counsel: "Be ruthless with yourself if you are given to talking about the experiences you have had. Faith that is sure of itself is not faith. Faith that is sure of God is the only faith there is."[2]

And that, don't you suppose, is the position Naaman eventually comes to? He has to admit he can't heal himself. He wouldn't be in Israel if he could. His destiny is not in his own hands. And he is sure the Israelite servant girl who recommended his journey to Israel has no ulterior motive. She really wants him well. The servants who have traveled with him are equally concerned about his well-being. And Elisha? I suspect Naaman still doesn't feel very good about him. But he is willing to humble himself before the prophet and his God if that's what it takes to be cured. The truth is, Naaman has learned the way of humility. If he is to get well, he has to have help. He is in no position to be choosy.

So the great general goes to the river.

Tune Up

1. In what situation in your life do you believe God is saying to you: "Verify if you must. But trust. Try it. See what happens." (For example, you may be struggling with obedience in loving a difficult person, giving sacrificially, giving up a habit.)

2. Through what very humble circumstances, persons, or media does God speak to people? How have you experienced this?

3. What do you see of trust and obedience in the life of Naaman's Hebrew servant girl who spoke up to save her master and whose character was so above board that her master didn't suspect her of any ulterior motive?

Trust and healing

Naaman's success story forces the issue that we are reading about with increasing frequency these days, the relationship of trust in God and healing. The century-old war between science and religion is abating. In many branches of science the practitioners are learning a new humility, bowing to the accumulating evidence that prayer, to select one example, does indeed affect healing and that church attendance (to select another) and better health go hand in hand.

It's the partnership that is receiving renewed emphasis today. Neither the so-called "spiritual healer" who dismisses scientific investigation and evidence nor the pompous scientist who categorically rejects all religious claims deserve a thoughtful hearing. I love the good-natured jab the French playwright Moliere takes at imperious doctors in his *"L'Amour Medecin,"* written in 1665. The situation is bleak.

A woman is ill. Four doctors are summoned. They come to the house, enter into private consultation with one another, but they discuss only their own affairs and not the condition of the unfortunate patient. The father insists they give him their decision and prescribe a remedy. His wish is their command. One prescribes an enema, another swears it will kill the patient. The renowned physicians cannot agree with one another. So the play continues until the patient recovers, but without taking any of their medicine. Her getting well without benefit of medical assistance infuriates the doctors: "It is better to die according to the rules," cries Dr. Bahys, "than to recover contrary to them."

Moliere was having fun at the medical men's expense. He enjoyed a good relationship with his personal doctor, yet he did so by following his own beneficial formula: "We reason with one another; he prescribes remedies; I omit to take them, and I recover."

As Moliere whimsically suggests, there is more to healing than medicine can control. It's this "more than" factor that has students of health taking a closer look at the role that trust in God plays. A Yankelovich Partners' survey at a recent meeting of the American Academy of Family Physicians found that 99 percent of these learned men and women are convinced religious belief can heal. Other results: 75 percent believe the prayers of others can help a patient's recovery, 38 percent believe faith healers can make people well.

Similar surveys have turned up equally fascinating statistics: 45 percent of drug and alcohol addicts recovered when faith in a supreme being was included in the recovery program. Without the faith factor, the recovery rate was 5 percent.

A study of 47,423 individuals in Washington County, Maryland, by Johns Hopkins researchers found that people who went to church at least once a week had the lowest mortality rates; those who never attended church had the highest.

Six or seven studies in the last 30 years have shown that religious commitment is associated with lower blood pressure.

A study of white males in rural Georgia found that religious belief even protected smokers. Those for whom religion was very important had a four times lower risk of hypertension than smokers who said it wasn't.

Researchers found that 88 percent of cancer patients who had religious faith found a better quality of life than those who did not.

A 1995 study at Dartmouth-Hitchcock Medical Center discovered that one of the best predictors of survival among 232 heart-surgery patients was the degree to which they drew comfort and strength from religious faith. Those without a religious faith had more than three times the death rate.

Men and women who attend church regularly have one-half the risk of dying from coronary-artery disease compared with those who do not.

A 1996 National Institute on Aging study of 4,000 elderly living at home in North Carolina found those who attend religious services are less depressed and physically healthier than those who do not.

Non-churchgoers have a four times higher suicide rate.

Harvard's Herbert Benson holds that "humans are actually engineered for religious faith." We are, he says, "wired for God."

Much more could be added, but this is enough. You could argue with some of these studies, pointing out that the definitions of supreme being and religious faith seem to be pretty vague. Granted. I didn't say that there weren't reasons to be cautious. (Remember Reagan: Trust but verify!) It does seem instructive, however, that the accumulating evidence from studies of all kinds points to the relationship between trust and healing. Hospitals are practicing good medicine when they provide spiritual assistance through a staff chaplain. Pastoral care goes hand in hand with medical assistance. One of the church's most important ministries takes place at a patient's bedside. Trusting God is a vital element in physical healing.

Naaman did the right thing. He trusted the word from the Lord. He humbled himself and obeyed. And he was healed.

Trust and rejoicing

While I was preparing to write this chapter on Naaman, our annual all-Lawson family vacation week rolled around. Once a year we come together from Oregon, Colorado, Arizona, and California, between twenty and thirty in all, meeting at a campsite large enough to accommodate us. Grandma and I preside over this rambunctious assembly of ten or so little ones and their assorted parents. We're water rats, so you'll find us swimming, water- and jet-skiing, wind-surfing, white water rafting, inflatable-kayaking, sand-digging, and enjoying whatever else we can find to do, including doing battle in some ferocious water fights. It's one great, glorious time.

If you look past the general hilarity and goodwill, though, you'll discover we're a family of self-admitted misfits.

My wife Joy is an exception. She's from a stable home, her parents married nearly sixty years. They aren't able to come to our vacations anymore because of the infirmities of age, but their mutual love still inspires. They are the model the rest of us couples hope to imitate.

My parents' marriage ended in divorce after nineteen years. In two generations, all the marriages in my family have been victimized by divorce. Joy and I are the only couple not having divorced or married someone divorced and that, I always quickly admit, is a tribute to her virtue and patience.

Our family consists of two biological daughters, their husbands and children, and several "adopted" kids, most of whom were with us on vacation. (When we were in Australia recently, friends gave us the descriptive word we've been searching for to describe these adoptees: they are our

"Velcro®"* kids. They stick! Never legally adopted, they are ours anyway.)

One Velcro® son came from a home in which the mother had been married five times (to say nothing of the other men in her life). His father was an alcoholic. He became "ours" as a teenager. He's still ours even though he's in his fifties now and an elder in his church.

Another Velcro® son also came from a family of multiple divorces. In his thirties now, he is in some ways more ours than theirs, a closeness made possible by our shared faith.

An adopted daughter (again, from a home in which she did not know her father and her mother had been married several times) and her husband (whom we think of as both our Velcro® son and our Velcro® son-in-law) are responsible for a couple of our favorite grandchildren (we don't have any other kind).

At the reunion were a family of four that we can claim only indirectly—they are the Velcro® kids and grandkids of our oldest Velcro® son. The tale the mother tells of her terrifying upbringing at the hands of a child-beating, drug-dealing father causes you to wonder how she became the beautiful person who blessed our gathering. I got a little insight when she told me of her belief in Christ.

Our two natural daughters would probably confess, if you pushed them, that they themselves are the scarred offspring of their scarred preacher father.

Fortunately, two of our dearest friends (and mine from my childhood), George and JoAnn, join us every year. They bring a touch of normality to the family, being two of the healthiest people we know, and must at times wonder about the rest of us.

There we are. Yet—remember what I said when I started talking about the family—our vacations are marked by

---

*"Velcro®" is a registered trademark of The Velcro Companies, Manchester, New Hampshire.

laughter, energy, playfulness, and love. If we were drinking people, you might have accused us sometimes of being drunk. We can be that boisterous. What you would see, however, isn't drink-induced abandon but love-filled joy. Are our reunions always perfect? No, we have our moments. Do we have any prickly personalities among us? Yes, mine most of all.

When the week was over, though, I realized that I had spent the whole week, whenever I had a free moment, giving thanks. For the privilege. All of us who are old enough to make the decision are in the Lord. All have been washed in the healing waters. All are filled with love and hope.

We are proof that trust leads to joy.

When Naaman returned to Elisha to give thanks for his healing, he tried to ply the prophet with gifts of gratitude. Elisha wouldn't accept a thing. God had healed. Elisha had done nothing. So Naaman did the next best thing. He transported as much Israelite dirt as a pair of mules could carry back to his home in Syria, "for your servant will never again make burnt offerings and sacrifices to any other god but the Lord" (2 Kings 5:15-17).

I understand, don't you? When the Lord heals you, you have to have some way to express your joy.

Tune Up

1. How are you thankful for times you've trusted God in the past?

2. In what ways do you admire Naaman?

3. How does trust often lead to healing? (Use the same examples, if you wish: healing of finances, health, relationships.)

---

[1]Ronald Reagan, *An American Life.* New York, et al: Simon and Schuster, 1990.

[2]Quoted in Os Guinness, *God in the Dark.* Wheaton: Crossway Books, 1996.

CHAPTER 4

THE WAY THROUGH DISOBEDIENCE

Jonah 1:1-17

"Why don't you preach a series of sermons on obedience?"
The question came almost out of nowhere. The chairman
of the elders and I were talking about a number of things,
reviewing the status of the church, planning some future ini-
tiatives. Then he abruptly switched the subject to my preaching. A quiet, meditative man, he was not given to telling his
pastor what he should say in the pulpit. This was the only
time we discussed the content of my sermons during his
three-year tenure. His desire, he made clear, was not for me
to "give it to them." It isn't unusual for church leaders, in
their frustration over the congregation's lethargy or sin, to
urge the preacher to blast away from the pulpit, giving the
people the kind of scolding they themselves would deliver if
they had pulpit privileges. That was the furthest thing from
the chairman's mind. As was characteristic of this spiritually
sensitive man, he was concerned about his own struggle to
obey. He confessed that he loved God (which I knew) and
wanted to serve him with all his heart (which I had seen for
years)—but inwardly he resisted completely surrendering
(which I did not know).

Would I help him—and incidentally the congregation—to
learn the way of obedience more perfectly?

That conversation has remained with me to this day. Even
after years of returning to his requested theme again and

again, I am not certain my sermons have helped him find peace on the subject. Nor have I quieted my own self-assertiveness, my irritating insistence on having my own way, even when it is not good for me. How I wish I could truthfully claim with the apostle Paul, "I am crucified with Christ: nevertheless I live; yet not I, but Christ liveth in me: and the life which I now live in the flesh I live by the faith of the Son of God, who loved me, and gave himself for me" (Galatians 2:20, KJV). I am not there yet. Neither is the chairman. But the struggle is not ours alone. Every conscientious believer must decide—and most of us have to return to the issue again and again—whose will is sovereign in my life, mine or God's?

Nowhere is this conflict of wills more dramatically acted out than in the book of Jonah. Mention Jonah's name and most of us think of a storm at sea and a prophet in the belly of a big fish. His is really, however, a tale of two roads: the Road to Nineveh (obedience and service) and the Road to Tarshish (disobedience and flight).

Jonah opts to flee.

Running from God

Why would any sane person deliberately defy God? If we could answer the question, we could tame our own rebelliousness. Stubborn independence almost seems to be bred into our genes, as proponents of the doctrine of original sin insist. If you believe as I do, however, that our defiance is not biologically determined but instead expresses our independent will, you won't be satisfied with merely blaming your ancestors for your waywardness.

Let's become more personal. Ask, as I often have had to, why do I consciously and deliberately do the opposite of what I know is God's will? There are several possible explanations, none satisfactory:

- Arrogance—I know better than God! (Do I really think this?)

- Preference—I simply do not desire what God wants for me or, as in Jonah's case, I do not desire what God wants for them (the Ninevites, whom God wants to save)!
- Independence—I want to be my own boss; I will not submit to any other authority, even the authority of God. (That this makes me my own god should cause me more discomfort than it does.)
- Self-image—Do I want to appear to be spineless, lacking in self-will, simply responding to orders? No way!
- Rebellion—It isn't that I won't take orders from God. I won't take orders from anybody. The world's out of joint. I will not conform. Period.

Tune Up

1. Maybe you've struggled with obedience and wished you had a magic button to make yourself obedient. Write a sentence to God expressing that struggle.

2. Look at the above list of reasons we disobey God. Circle the one that has gotten you into the most trouble.

3. Look at the list again. The wording is very strong. Maybe you would describe yourself with milder words, such as withdrawn, displeased, or simply forgetful (of obedience). How are these, too, forms of rebellion?

4. Look at the list a last time. Put a square around the issues in which you have made progress recently. Thank God for that in the space below.

In moments of introspection we identify all too well with Jonah, having been guilty of all of the above and more. In my case, someone might call it the Little Man Syndrome, this drive to be my own person, to do my own thing, to take orders from no one. My spiritual journey through life has been one of constantly having to learn the lessons of submission. Many temptations pass by without my giving them a second glance, but the temptation to elbow God's will aside in favor of my own just will not leave me alone. Sound familiar?

For this reason I confess to understanding Jonah far better than I do persons of more obedient temperament. One of Jimmy Carter's models, for example, seems almost unbelievable to me. The former president calls Judge Elbert Tuttle "one of the great jurists of our country." President Dwight Eisenhower appointed him to the bench, where

Judge Tuttle handed down what Mr. Carter says were "some of the most definitive and courageous rulings" during Georgia's turbulent civil-rights struggle. He is obviously a man of courage and rectitude. Walter Cronkite interviewed Judge Tuttle when he retired, asking him, among other questions, "Judge Tuttle, I understand you've never drunk whiskey."

"That's right, I've never in my life tasted an alcoholic drink."

"Why not?"

"Because my mama told me not to."[1]

President Carter admires the judge's acquiescence to his mother's will. I marvel at it. Tuttle made a lifelong practice of virtue—not the virtue of abstinence, which is admirable in itself, but the greater virtue of obedience. My curiosity, restlessness, and, yes, self-assertiveness would have left me unsatisfied until I had tasted the forbidden drink if for no other reason than to try to figure out what my mother had against it. The result, I do not boast to admit, is that the good judge is a far more reliable man than I.

Or than Jonah. There is no question in his mind what God wants him to do. For reasons of his own, he will not.

His stubbornness reminds me of a little lesson on delegation that I read a number of years ago. Some sage had concluded that there are three ways to get something done:

1. Do it yourself.
2. Hire someone else to do it.
3. Forbid your kids to do it.

There is something of the rebellious kid in Jonah, although by my amateur psychologizing, he should have felt insulted by God's demands. He has his reason—and his reason is that he hates the Ninevites. He considers himself a better man than any of them. His prejudice runs so deep he has no trouble consigning the entire population to destruction rather than to stoop to save a one of them. It is a matter of principle with him.

George Bernard Shaw, the famous Irish playwright, comments somewhere about a man who resigned his seat in parliament rather than compromise his principle. Shaw is not impressed. He thinks Joe could have risked "just a speck or two on those white robes of his" on behalf of "the millions of poor devils who cannot afford any character at all because they have no friends in parliament," As far as Shaw is concerned, Joe is a "moral dandy" a "spiritual toff." Why shouldn't Joe risk his soul occasionally like everyone else, he wonders.

Not a bad question for Jonah, either.

Consequence of the flight

Read the four chapters of Jonah. Without the last chapter you will have difficulty understanding the first. Jonah runs because he fears that if he obeys the Lord and preaches in Nineveh, the people he despises will be saved. Their salvation is what God wants. That is precisely what Jonah does not want. He has learned, undoubtedly, what Peter discovered centuries later, but Jonah does not approve: "The Lord is not slow in keeping his promise, as some understand slowness. He is patient with you, not wanting anyone to perish, but everyone to come to repentance" (2 Peter 3:9).

In God's challenge to Jonah we get a foreshadowing of the mission of another, far greater Preacher to come. He, too, was sent to a people steeped in sin and was sent for the same reason: that they might not die in that condition. "For God so loved the world that he gave his one and only Son, that whoever believes in him shall not perish but have eternal life. For God did not send his Son into the world to condemn the world, but to save the world through him" (John 3:16, 17).

Even though the language in Jonah's commission sounds negative ("Go to the great city of Nineveh and preach against it, because its wickedness has come up before me"), God's purposes are positive. In this case, "against" is good: God is against sin, against the Ninevites' "lifestyle" (as we would call it today), and against their destiny (destruction lies ahead if they do not change), but He is for the citizens of that wicked city. He does not want them to perish.

So to escape God's contradicting love, Jonah flees.

The responsibility for the flight

On the one hand, Jonah accepts the blame for his decision. With the storm raging and the boat in serious danger, he admits to the captain, "I know that it is my fault that this great storm has come upon you." They're all having to pay for his disobedience. He urges them to cast him overboard, so at least they will be safe.

On the other hand, Jonah believes none of this would have happened if God had just left him alone. Listen to his lament in the second chapter, uttered, we are told, from inside the fish. *"You* hurled me into the deep, into the very heart of the seas, and the currents swirled about me; all *your* waves and breakers swept over me. . . . I have been banished from your sight [by *you,* God]. . . . The engulfing waters threatened me, the deep surrounded me; seaweed was wrapped around my head. To the roots of the mountains I sank down; the earth beneath barred me in forever. [And all these move at *your* command!]"

He is a victim of God's plan, as far as Jonah is concerned.

If it were not for God, Jonah would not have to flee aboard the doomed (because of God, again) ship and would not now be trapped inside the fish. God's, then, is the responsibility for the flight—but God's also, Jonah is forced to concede, is the grace that saves:

"But you brought my life up from the pit, O Lord my God. When my life was ebbing away, I remembered you, Lord, and my prayer rose to you, to your holy temple. Those who cling to worthless idols forfeit the grace that could be theirs. But I, with a song of thanksgiving, will sacrifice to you. What I have vowed I will make good. Salvation comes from the Lord."

We are introduced, then, in the midst of the second chapter's praise-lament, to a newly obedient Jonah: "yet I will look again toward your holy temple." The Lord takes the penitent preacher at his word: "And the Lord commanded the fish, and it vomited Jonah onto dry land." He is now ready for Nineveh.

Tune Up

1. Most of us have a "rebellious kid" in us. How do you usually deal with that inner "rebellious kid"?

2. What do you say to a person such as Jonah who doesn't want to do the right thing because it somehow feels morally wrong? (For example, being kind to a cruel person or being friendly to someone your friend dislikes.)

3. How do you explain Jonah's mixed heart—he felt like a victim, but also knew he needed God's grace?

I understand there's a tradition in Islam, reported by 'Umar, the second Caliph, that an angel (Gabriel, we are told) appeared once before the Prophet Muhammad. Seating himself directly opposite the prophet and placing his palms on the prophet's thighs, he said, "O Muhammad, tell me what is the surrender unto God (al-islam)." The prophet answered, "The surrender is that thou shouldst testify that there is no god but God and that Muhammad is God's Apostle, that thou shouldst perform the prayer, bestow the alms, fast Ramadan and make, if thou canst, the pilgrimage to the Holy House."

The angel said, "Thou hast spoken truly."[2]

When I first learned of this tradition, I marveled at the simplicity that seems to this outsider to characterize the Islamic faith. (I am certain there is much, much more to be understood, but I am merely reacting to the little I have been taught about it.) This tradition suggests that the essence of Islamic faith is found in a couple of facts to be believed (God is One and Muhammad is his apostle) and a few rituals to be observed.

As I said, I am undoubtedly oversimplifying.

In a sense, the Christian faith is simple also—but oh how difficult the application! What God desires of us is obedience. Not ritual, but obedience. The prophet Micah captures this in his famous summary statement often quoted by Christian preachers, "He has showed you, O man, what is good. And what does the Lord require of you? To act justly and to love mercy and to walk humbly with your God" (Micah 6:8). Easy to quote, but very difficult to apply. Jonah could have written these words, but he would have had a great deal to say from personal experience about what it means to walk humbly with God. Not the performing of certain ritual acts, but the obeying of God's undisputed will. That is obedience.

Running toward Tarshish

The Scripture doesn't explain why Jonah makes Tarshish his destination. We suspect it has one overriding virtue. It is as far away from Nineveh as Jonah can flee. When you are escaping your God-directed destiny, almost anywhere looks better than Nineveh.

But the road to Tarshish (disobedience, flight) is the road to destruction. Rebellion feels so good. Who doesn't enjoy "doing your own thing," "calling your own shots," "defying the authorities"? Who hasn't had to pay the price?

One man paid the ultimate price. In Yosemite National Park a French visitor was swimming in a pool above a 600-foot waterfall when he slipped on the rocks, got caught in a strong current, and was pulled over the edge of the falls to his death below. A photograph taken before the incident survived him. In it he posed next to a sign that stated, "If you Swim Here You Will Die." So he swam. It must have been exhilarating, his defiance of authority. The sign, of course, was meant for other people. Unfortunately, it told the truth.

Jan Karon picks up on this theme of running from authority (ultimate authority: God) in *At Home in Mitford*. The old curmudgeon Russell Jacks, fighting for his life, is also fighting his nurse Betty. When the visiting rector scolds him, Russell turns surprisingly contrite. "You're right, Father, you're dead right, an' I know it. I'm th' roughest ol' cob you ever seen when it comes t' mindin.' That's why I've fought th' Lord s'long, it meant mindin' 'im if I was t' foller 'im. It's about wore me out, fightin' 'im. Not t' say I don't respect 'im, I do. But I don't want t' mind 'im."

Ms. Karon editorializes, "The uneducated Russell Jacks, thought the rector, had just put the taproot cause of the world's ills into a few precise words."[3]

Jesus considers "mindin'" the essence of discipleship. He ties it to a cross, so there will be no misunderstanding the cost of obedience: "If anyone would come after me, he must deny himself and take up his cross and follow me. For whoever wants to save his life will lose it, but whoever loses his life for me will find it" (Matthew 16:24, 25). Obedience is a life-and-death matter and self-denial is its requisite. Boasting of one's willfulness, parading one's stubborn egoism while refusing to bow the knee to any higher authority is the surefire formula for self-destruction. In Nineveh Jonah would have to give up his self-centeredness but in the process he would save a city and himself; in Tarshish, however—well, fortunately Jonah doesn't have to find out what awaits him there. We know, though. He would find himself, as he wanted, as far from God's will as possible. And if Jesus is right, having found himself he would lose everything.

Consequences of running

When you are running away from God's call, people get hurt. We usually do not notice the effect of our selfishness, wrapped up as we are in ourselves. The alcoholic has a vague idea of the grief the loved ones suffer, but isn't sufficiently aware to change. What damage is wrought by addicts of every kind, by bullheaded children who stomp on their parents' dreams, by single-minded careerists determined to climb the corporate ladder no matter who else gets hurt— and by former believers who, in their revolt against God, heap ridicule and scorn on the poor benighted souls who chose to worship and obey.

On vacation one of our daughters passed on a joke she had heard somewhere: "What do you do when a shark attacks?" Our guesses were wide of the mark. "You stab your buddy!" she exclaimed.

As a joke, it's a crowd pleaser. As a philosophy of life, it's cruel. As a touch of reality, it's too accurate.

Jonah ran. His fellow sailors suffered. Had he kept running, Nineveh would have been lost. Consequences.

Tune Up

1. In what areas are you most likely to "do your own thing" or "call your own shots"?

2. Remembering that obedience results in discipleship and disobedience results in self-destruction, name some things that would be attractive about being discipled to Jesus. How would a person be better off?

Who's responsible for his escape to Tarshish?

At last Jonah has to accept the responsibility. He has caused the storm. Because of him, the sailors fear there will be blood on their hands. They don't want the guilt of tossing him overboard. "Instead, the men did their best to row back to land. But they could not, for the sea grew even wilder than before." Realizing there is no escaping Jonah's fate unless they separate themselves from him, "they cried to the Lord, 'O Lord, please do not let us die for taking this man's life. Do not hold us accountable for killing an innocent man, for you, O Lord, have done as you pleased.'"

"An innocent man." From their perspective, perhaps. He has done them no visible harm. They do not consider him a criminal, a fugitive from justice.

But "innocent"? In their prayer we find the distinction between "not guilty" and "innocent." In a court of law these may be opposite pleas. But here Jonah's being "innocent" of any man-made crime does not make him "not guilty" in God's court.

It's a distinction Jonah understands. "I know that it is my fault that this great storm has come upon you." Now there is hope for Jonah. He has accepted responsibility.

The theologian Emil Brunner places sin and irresponsibility in the same category. One defines the other. Noting that man "does not live in a truly responsible manner," Brunner insists that he "lives in that irresponsibility and in that misunderstanding of responsibility which the Bible calls 'sin' and 'life under the law.'" He then boldly states, "True responsibility is the same as true humanity."[4] Jonah, so long as he shirks his responsibility before God, is acting inhumanely in regard to the Ninevites and the sailors. Once he faces up to his duty, the sailors initially and Nineveh ultimately benefit. Jonah has become, in Brunner's terms, human.

What is never an issue in Jonah's adventure is his faith. Whether he's running toward Tarshish or, at last, doing his duty in Nineveh, Jonah never doubts God's existence. God is real, powerful, even overwhelming. The question never is, "Is there a God?" The real question is, "Shall I let the real God be my personal God?" Or, more succinctly, "Shall I live for Him?"

This is the question in Ernest H. Crosby's poem:

> So he died for his faith. That is fine—
>   More than most of us do.
> But say, can you add to that line
>   That he lived for it, too?
> In his death he bore witness at last
>   As a martyr to truth.
> Did his life do the same in the past
>   From the days of his youth?

> It is easy to die. Men have died
> > For a wish or a whim—
> From bravado or passion or pride.
> > Was it harder for him?
> But to live: every day to live out
> > All the truth that he dreamt,
> While his friends met his conduct with doubt,
> > And the world with contempt—
> Was it thus that he plodded ahead,
> > Never turning aside?
> Then we'll talk of the life that he led.
> > Never mind how he died.[5]

Which is the conclusion of the matter, isn't it? We don't know about Jonah's death. We have been studying his near-death, his miraculous rescue from the waters of disobedience. We find we cannot even commend him for bringing the story to a happy conclusion. Even at the end he is pouting before God. Pouting, disappointed, but obedient.

I wish we could admire Jonah more. But then, are you like me in wishing you could admire yourself more? Obviously, in studying Jonah we have not learned how to reach the heights of spiritual maturity. We have, though, become persuaded of the necessity of at least one basic ingredient, the essential first step toward maturity. We have learned to obey.

For that, for now, we can be thankful.

Tune Up

1. What does it tell us about Jonah that he didn't agree with the crew that he was an innocent person?

2. These questions, "Shall I let the real God be my personal God? Shall I live for Him?" are calls to discipleship. What positive steps (if any) toward discipleship to Jesus have you made recently?

3. As you view the ups and downs of Jonah's life, do you see yourself? Why or why not?

[1]Jimmy Carter, *Living Faith.* New York: Times Books, 1996.

[2]*The World Treasury of Modern Religious Thought,* ed. Jaroslav Pelikan. Boston, et al: Little, Brown and Company.

[3]Jan Karon, *At Home in Mitford.* New York: Penguin Books, 1994.

[4]Emil Brunner, *Man in Revolt.* Philadelphia: Westminster Press, 1939.

[5]From Robert E. Speer, *Five Minutes a Day.* Philadelphia: Westminster Press, 1929.

CHAPTER 5

THE WAY OUT OF A LIONS' DEN

Daniel 6:1-28

You've been there. You feel trapped—you may be trapped. You can't see any way out. There is no escape. Your temples are pounding, your breathing is tortured, you can't talk yourself into calming down. Then as if by instinct, you do the only possible thing. You pray. And you live to tell about it.

You probably aren't well acquainted with the ways of lions, but about prayer you do know a thing or two because, as I said, you've been there. You can identify with Daniel. You've been locked up with your own lions. And you prayed.

I approach the subject of prayer with hesitation. It seems so presumptuous of me to write as if I were some kind of authority, I, whose prayer life is no more remarkable than anyone else's, whose answers have often been quite other than what I hoped for. As I try to pull my thoughts together for this chapter I feel like the bishop in one of Leo Tolstoy's stories. Three hermits lived an isolated but godly existence on an island. They were praying men, but their prayers were very simple, as were the men. "We are three; you are three; have mercy on us. Amen." So they prayed. Yet miracles sometimes happened. God honored their artless prayers.

When the bishop learned of the gentle hermits with their trusting faith, he was impressed. He wanted to help them, believing they would profit from guidance in proper prayer.

Undoubtedly congratulating himself for his missionary zeal, he sailed to their small island and undertook their instruction. When he had done his best by them, he set sail for home, pleased he had been the instrument of their enlightenment.

Sailing away, however, he suddenly spotted off the stern of the ship a huge ball of light skimming across the ocean, coming closer and closer until he could see in the light his three hermits running on top of the water. They boarded the ship and spoke directly—and apologetically—to the bishop. "We are so sorry," they said, "but we have forgotten some of your teaching. Would you please instruct us again?"

The ecclesiastical leader shook his head. It was his turn to apologize. "Forget everything I have taught you and continue to pray in your old way."

He had met his betters. So have I.

For people like me, then, Daniel's sojourn in the lions' den is worthy of close scrutiny—not for the lions, but for some basic lessons in prayer. Here's the first one.

Your committed prayer life sustains you.

I first wrote ". . . sustains you in trouble," but scratched it out. Prayer does, of course, bolster our flagging spirits and threatened wills, but the sentence was too limiting. At least as important is the truth that your committed prayer life sustains you in prosperity as well. Daniel did not suddenly feel an urge to begin communicating with God after he was tossed into the lions' den. He was at the pinnacle of his career—the kingdom's top administrator. His daily calendar was crammed with demands for his attention, but he did not neglect his spiritual disciplines. "Then they [Daniel's enemies] said to the king, 'Daniel, who is one of the exiles from Judah, pays no attention to you, O king, or to the decree you put in writing. He still prays three times a day' [as he had always done, even before Darius succumbed to his advisers' absurd proposal that] 'anyone who prays to any god or man during the next thirty days, except to you, O king, shall be thrown into the lions' den.'"

His praying now was not to defy Darius's decree, or to flaunt his independence, or to challenge his adversaries. He was merely doing what he had always done. He practiced the discipline that the apostle Paul later challenged Christians to observe. He prayed "without ceasing" (1 Thessalonians 5:17, KJV). In addition to the praise and thanksgiving at the heart of every believer's conversations with God, Daniel laid his administrative challenges before the Lord, seeking wisdom, discernment, patience, and yes, protection, from the mood swings and arbitrary whims of his sovereign. He prayed when all was well. Having for so long relied on God's providential care, Daniel did not hesitate to seek Him when the king's favor was withdrawn.

A good friend of mine, a longtime member of Alcoholics Anonymous, recently handed me a slip on which he had copied a thought from the AA meditation book: "Prayer doesn't change God's attitude toward me; it changes my attitude toward God." He has lived by these lines, he said, for years. Regular, sustaining prayer prepares the believer for whatever. When you walk with God in trust and expectancy at the top, you'll find Him close and faithful when you find yourself at the bottom.

Tune Up

1. Try to name a time when you were locked up with your own "lions" and then saw the light of day.

2. What would cause a man at the pinnacle of his career who had a daily calendar crammed with demands to take time out to pray three times a day?

3. Consider this phrase in light of some matter in your life about which you have prayed little or not at all: "Prayer doesn't change God's attitude toward me; it changes my attitude toward God."

Terry Anderson, one of America's hostages in the Middle East, discovered that even a nominal Christian who has pretty much ignored God for years can find courage and strength through prayer. Upon his release from imprisonment (much of it in solitary confinement), Anderson published his story. His book includes a powerful testimony to prayer, in this case the prayer of an indifferent believer, one not certain God was hearing because of the author's own sense of unworthiness. He dared to ask God for help when "there's no reason why You should." What right did he, Anderson, have to request anything of the One whom he had so long ignored? His prayer was terse: "You say you love me. So help me." He received no flash of lightning, no chains falling from his wrists. But, he could testify, "the hours are endured, the days gotten through. And the nights are spent in prayer, and thought, and the effort to get back to that place [of peace]." Of that place he writes,

No flawed man, beset by passion
can hope to hold it long,
though some rare souls
bathe often in its glow.
For most, a light
infrequent touch, perhaps
just once a life,
must be enough.

What happened to Anderson was enough to sustain him. When he reached that place of peace, he says, "into / exhausted calm comes a presence, / soft, almost timorously, / of warmth and light and love."[1]

His language borders on the mystical. I include it here because it speaks for many of us who, after laborious praying, after years of almost rote repetition or anxious searching, have felt that presence and been embraced in "warmth and light and love." It does not come to the casual ritualist, the gasping pray-er-on-the-run. As Sheila Cassia writes in her *Prayer for Pilgrims,* "We should think of prayer as an art which will only develop with care and perseverance and continued practice throughout our lifetime."[2]

When I read Anderson's book I remembered the beautiful words of John Greenleaf Whittier that we used to sing in my home church.

Drop Thy still dews of quietness,
   Till all our strivings cease;
Take from our souls the strain and stress,
   And let our ordered lives confess
The beauty of Thy peace.

Breathe through the heats of our desire
   Thy coolness and Thy balm;
Let sense be dumb, let flesh retire;
   Speak through the earthquake, wind, and fire,
O still small Voice of calm!

        ("Dear Lord and Father of Mankind")

That kind of prayer sustains us. So in all things, at all times, we pray.

> In the same way, the Spirit helps us in our weakness. We do not know what we ought to pray for, but the Spirit himself intercedes for us with groans that words cannot express. And he who searches our hearts knows the mind of the Spirit, because the Spirit intercedes for the saints in accordance with God's will. And we know that in all things God works for the good of those who love him, who have been called according to his purpose.
>
> Romans 8:26-28

Tune Up

1. If others asked you how they could pray in such a way that they would experience the embrace of "warmth and light and love," what would you say?

2. Underline any words in the hymn that describe your prayers now or how you would like for your prayers to be.

3. Since Scripture says the Spirit helps us in our weakness (Romans 8:26), how would you ask God to let the Spirit help you in your prayer?

Your prayer life can get you into a heap of trouble.

The second lesson often comes as a surprise to young believers, especially if they are turning to the Lord as a refuge from marital, financial, unemployment, abuse, or other threatening problems. "Surely if I pray, God will protect me from trouble, won't He?" They have come to Him because they heard and accepted the many assurances the Bible provides. Then, when trouble hits again, they don't know what to think. "What about all the scriptural promises to ask for whatever we want and God will give it to us? Well, I'm asking!" Well-meaning teachers compound this perplexity by insisting that people need only take their concerns to the Lord and He will take care of them. "Don't worry, just pray."

How do they explain Daniel, these glib teachers? It was because he was so ardent in prayer that he found himself in trouble. You can't rise as high as Daniel rose in Darius's government without kindling jealousy. Daniel's competitors were watching his every move, yearning for a misstep. Nobody ever tells you, while cheering you on, goading you to go out and make a name for yourself, that if you succeed you'll be the natural prey of the envious, the mediocre, the ambitious. Daniel's spies' diligence paid off handsomely. They could not find any corruption or negligence in him, but they had discovered the source of his strength. He prayed. To the wrong god.

They had their man. With malevolent skill they manipu-
lated their egotistical king. An oriental despot, Darius ruled
by decree. His word was law, his person sacred, his will
absolute. When his court sycophants proposed a decree
declaring a special season in his honor, he could not resist.
"Anyone who prays to any god or man . . . except to you, O
king, shall be thrown into the lions' den." Let it be done!

The trap was set. Their prey was doomed. "Now when
Daniel learned that the decree had been published, he went
home to his upstairs room where the windows opened
toward Jerusalem. Three times a day he got down on his
knees and prayed, *giving thanks to his God, just as he had
done before."*

What choice did he have? He served a higher authority
than Darius.

If you have ever held an administrative position, you can
sympathize with Daniel. Nor are administrators unique in
this matter. What politician, businessman, teacher, worker,
parent—for that matter, who else hasn't been caught in the
squeeze between what superiors require of you and what
your God-directed conscience requires? Daniel surely went
to his room wondering when—not if—he would be arrested.
But the certain knowledge of his fate did not stop his
prayers.

Enemies. They loom large in the Bible. It's an eye-opening
experience to pick up a Bible concordance and search for
verses containing the words "enemies" or "enemy." You
quickly lose count of the entries. Only one conclusion is
possible. This earth is a hostile place, and our greatest danger is other members of the human family.

His words were his own, but Daniel's prayer undoubtedly
echoed the sentiments of David's, "In you I trust, O my
God. Do not let me be put to shame, nor let my enemies
triumph over me" (Psalm 25:2). Who hasn't uttered a
similar plea?

In small ways and large, then, the faithful pray-er can
expect trouble. We pray in trouble, we certainly pray for

help to get out of trouble, and we sometimes pray into trouble, as Daniel did. I love the way an old farmer handled his prayer-induced annoyance in Gerald Kennedy's story. The old man came to the city to buy his supplies. His business finished, he went to a restaurant for lunch, bowed his head and thanked God for his food. Some smart alecks, watching his simple act of piety from a nearby table, made sport of him. "Hey, farmer, does everyone do that out your way?" Unruffled, he quietly replied, "No, son. The pigs don't."[3]

I've chuckled over the story for years, but I've also wondered. What happened next? Do you imagine the hecklers laughed good-naturedly at his riposte? Or did the atmosphere suddenly turn cold, threatening?

In the Christian Endeavor meetings of my youth we often sang,

> I'll go where You want me to go, dear Lord,
> O'er mountain, or plain, or sea.
> I'll say what You want me to say, dear Lord,
> I'll be what You want me to be.

It's a prayer, this song, and it makes a radical promise. I sang with sincerity. In those days I was preparing to offer myself to the mission service. Only in later years did I come to understand that God accepted my offer. He never sent me to Africa, but he has sent me all around the United States. More importantly, he sent me to be a member of the clean-up committee, and to apologize when I was wrong (and when I wasn't), and to make myself unpopular by taking some moral stands or opposing some powerful leaders. He has heard me pray not my will, but thine be done and sent me to do it. And I have frequently found myself in trouble.

But then, Jesus also prayed. And His answer was a cross. Trouble.

Tune Up

1. How does it make you feel that Daniel found himself in trouble because he was so ardent in prayer?

2. What exactly can we pray when praying for our "enemies" (difficult people, people who pick on us, people who disagree disagreeably)?

Your God-service makes all your other service more valuable.

Admittedly, Daniel possessed extraordinary gifts of administration and leadership. Darius rewarded them with high office. What the king did not understand or would not admit was that Daniel would not have been the man he was apart from his spiritual disciplines. He could not neglect his prayer regimen and be the man Darius respected. His allegiance to God strengthened his character and organized his priorities. Prayer plus competence generates valuable service. What Darius appreciated in Daniel was his reliable proficiency; what he did not get from his chief administrator was mere subservience. A lesser man than Daniel would have obeyed the decree, fearing to lose his job if he violated his king's explicit order. But then a lesser man could always be counted on to do what Darius wanted, not what Darius needed. That's the difference between genuine service and mere servility.

Hence Darius's distress when he learned that his stupid decree would cost him his best man. "When the king heard this, he was greatly distressed; he was determined to rescue Daniel and made every effort until sundown to save him." Here's the rub with being king. You must be obeyed. Your word is law. Darius had spoken; his decree was irrevocable, as his unctuous, scheming courtiers were quick to remind him: "Then the men went as a group to the king and said to him, 'Remember, O king, that according to the law of the Medes and Persians no decree or edict that the king issues can be changed.'"

He was stuck. "So the king gave the order, and they brought Daniel and threw him into the lions' den. The king said to Daniel, *'May your God, whom you serve continually, rescue you!'*"

That was it. The consequences were out of the king's hands, and in God's. Unable to do anything else, Darius paced. "Then the king returned to his palace and spent the night without eating and without any entertainment being brought to him. And he could not sleep." The lions' den was no place for a trusted administrator. Even a king knows that. This king's great loss could be avoided only through the power of Daniel's God. You can bet Darius hoped that Daniel did the right thing when he defied the decree; for once, the king would be glad to acknowledge a power greater than his own.

My emphasis here on Darius's high appraisal of Daniel's worth could be misinterpreted. I am not suggesting that if you pray your boss will be bound to value you more highly or that your prayers will suddenly transform you into a more competent employee. No, Daniel's gift was administration; its source was God-given ability plus his own hard work and application. My point is that his solid allegiance to God expressed in his disciplined prayer life (from which he would not be turned in spite of the cost) enhanced his value to Darius. He could offer his king competence plus personal integrity based on faithfulness to God. He was worth more to Darius because he served someone other than Darius; his primary loyalty was to God, in whose name and for whose sake he was serving the king. And God's standards were far higher, more demanding, than the king's. Thus Daniel's God-service made his king-service all the more valuable.

Michael Novak, an American Catholic lay theologian and philosopher, comes to my rescue here. He defines prayer as "penetrating through phantasy to reality and gathering courage to act."[4] Prayer enabled Daniel to see through the intrigues and illusions of court life to the realities demanding his unbiased—and incorruptible—attention.

May God grant us more Daniels in high places!

Daniel's God can deliver you from the lions' den.

The climax of the story, of course, is Daniel's deliverance. The moral is found in the king's astonished reaction when he sees Daniel alive and unharmed. Such an event calls for (you guessed it) another decree.

But first, let's read the rest of the story:

> At the first light of dawn, the king got up and hurried to the lions' den. When he came near the den, he called to Daniel in an anguished voice, "Daniel, *servant of the living God,* has your God, whom you serve continually, been able to rescue you from the lions?"
>
> Daniel answered, "O king, live forever! My God sent his angel, and he shut the mouths of the lions. They have not hurt me, because I was found innocent in his sight. Nor have I ever done any wrong before you, O king."
>
> The king was overjoyed and gave orders to lift Daniel out of the den. And when Daniel was lifted from the den, no wound was found on him, because he had trusted in his God.
>
> At the king's command, the men who had falsely accused Daniel were brought in and thrown into the lions' den, along with their wives and children. And before they reached the floor of the den, the lions overpowered them and crushed all their bones.

> Then King Darius wrote to all the peoples, nations and
> men of every language throughout the land: "May you
> prosper greatly!"
>
> Daniel 6:19-25

We might want to take issue with the recorded language
on a minor point. The men hadn't actually falsely accused
Daniel, had they? They had accurately accused him. He was
guilty of defying the king's decree. He did pray to his own
God rather than to the king. They properly charged him with
unlawful action; they wrongfully impugned his motives, but
that is quite another thing.

As I said, it is a minor point. Sadly, the men and their
families paid dearly for their treachery. The king, on the
other hand, was in a mood to celebrate. His treasured administrator, counselor, and confidant had been spared. (You can't
help thinking, can you, of the father of the prodigal son in
Jesus' story who could barely contain himself because his
son "who was dead" is now "alive"?)

So, predictably, the rejoicing king issues another decree:

> I issue a decree that in every part of my kingdom people
> must fear and reverence the God of Daniel. For he is the
> living God and he endures forever; his kingdom will not be
> destroyed, his dominion will never end. He rescues and he
> saves; he performs signs and wonders in the heavens and on
> the earth. He has rescued Daniel from the power of the lions.
>
> Daniel 6:26, 27

Madeleine L'Engle tells of another kind of rescue. Her
friend Laryn leads conferences around the country, which
means she spends many nights alone in motel rooms. On one
such night she was preparing for bed when she received an
obscene phone call. Not just once, but twice more. Many
women would have been petrified alone, away from home,
in a strange motel, with someone having access to her room
number. Laryn didn't panic, though. On the last call she
calmly responded to her telephonic intruder, "I'm really

worried about you. I think you must be very lonely. What I would like to do with you is pray with you, right now . . ."
Click.

She slept in peace that night.[5]

Is deliverance (when alone and threatened in a motel room or in a lions' den) guaranteed to a believer? No. But I take solace in Karl Barth's insight: "To clasp the hands in prayer is the beginning of an uprising against the disorder of the world."[6] Instructive, isn't it, that Daniel immediately turned to prayer when faced with his king's foolish decree? When his world suddenly fell into disorder, he clasped his hands in "the beginning of an uprising."

How do we handle the disorder—the foolishness, the stupidity, the evil of our world? Go along? Close our eyes? Mount a soapbox and harangue against it? Quietly, personally work to subvert it?

Karl Barth is on to something. We can pray.

It isn't everything, but it's a beginning.

And, as Darius discovered, the answer can be astonishing.

Tune Up

1. "Daniel would not have been the man he was apart from his spiritual disciplines. . . . Prayer plus competence generates valuable service." In what ways might you be a better employee, spouse, parent, child if you were more spiritually disciplined?

2. What does Daniel's stepping back in a situation out of his control say to you?

3. In what situation (a job, a volunteer position, a relationship) would it help you to see God as your ultimate supervisor, and your best preparation to be prayer?

4. What disorder in this world—foolishness, evil, chaos—would you do well to talk or worry less about and pray more?

[1]Terry Anderson, *Den of Lions*. New York: Ballantine, 1994.

[2]Quoted in Philip Toynbee, *End of a Journey*. London: Bloomsbury Pub. Co., 1988.

[3]Gerald Kennedy, *Witnesses of the Spirit*. Nashville: The Upper Room, 1961.

[4]Michael Novak, *A Time to Build*. New York: Macmillan, 1967.

[5]Madeleine L'Engle, *The Rock That Is Higher*. Wheaton, Illinois: Harold Shaw Publishers, 1993.

[6]Quoted by Richard J. Foster, *Prayer*. New York: HarperCollins, 1992.

THE WAY THROUGH SIN

Matthew 3:1-17

The disgruntled parishioner's letter could not be misunderstood. As a prophet I was a failure. With our nation suffering unprecedented moral decay—AIDS, homosexuality, abortion, pornography, failure of the family, crime in the streets, immorality in the White House, and ineptitude in the Congress, to name only the most obvious issues—my pulpit had been cowardly silent. How could I call myself the spiritual leader of the church when I was apparently so indifferent to these political and moral issues? How did I expect my people to conduct themselves as Christians if I did not spell out in unmistakable detail precisely what they were to believe and how they were to act on each topic?

The same day I received that letter I also read through Sunday morning's registration cards. One stood out: "Central Christian has turned my life around." Written by a young Christian, this card gave me the ammunition I needed for my critic.

In the course of a 40-year ministry I have never been without such faultfinders. Urging me to mobilize church members against godless Communism, government-ordered busing, flag-burning, convenience store sales of soft-porn magazines, the intrigues of the Trilateral Commission, proliferation of satanic numbers (telephone, zip codes, social security, and so on) by means of which a worldwide dictator could gain control, these well-intentioned crusaders would have me convert the church into a forum for political indoctrination and social action.

My critics accuse me and the church I serve justly. We have repeatedly refused to be stampeded into yet another campaign on still another social ill, worthy of our attention though it is. It has been our conviction that more attention is not what most of these inflammatory issues have needed. Thanks to the media and politicians and crusading ministers and various other propagandists, the population at large has not been lacking either information or admonishing.

But our church leaders have cautioned me against jumping into such campaigns, urging me instead to pursue my calling as a proclaimer of the gospel. We have agreed that our task is to turn lives around. Our inspiration is the New Testament church which served the turbulent, equally sinful first century and followed a master who came not to wrest control from any human government but to establish a kingdom not entirely of this world. Jesus did not hand His church a political agenda but a spiritual, life-changing one. Although social injustice cried out on every hand, He focused His ministry on transforming the persons who would in turn right social wrongs. Hence when He commenced His ministry, He echoed the preaching of His cousin John the Baptist: "Repent, for the kingdom of heaven is near." As a treatment for individual and social ills, any other medicine addresses symptoms but does not effect a lasting cure. The ultimate solution is to put detoured lives back on the road to life.

Throughout this series of studies we have been investigating what these turned-around lives look like. Each chapter examines a facet of a person's spiritual journey. The title of Willie Nelson's popular song has come to mind often, but with new meaning: "On the Road Again." On the road again, but not toward the same destination—and not as the same traveler. Not only is the direction different (from Hell-bent to Heaven-bound), but so is the person. It is this difference that we want to comprehend more fully. Making this difference in people's lives is what motivates John the Baptist.

We look in at the high point of John's ministry. We are immediately impressed by John's boldness in scolding the sinners in his congregation ("you brood of vipers"). On closer examination, though, we realize that it isn't righteous indignation that bolsters John's audacity. He hasn't been called merely to fulminate against sins and sinners. He is preparing people to meet their God. He's driven by a divinely-inspired desire to turn them around, to help them change their way of thinking about themselves and about God, to convince them their security is not in their descent from Abraham ("We have Abraham as our father"), and to get them ready to follow the Messiah. That's a big enough assignment for any preacher, and one far more important than assailing the popular social problems of one's time.

Tune Up

1. When has God used you (even in a small way) to put a detoured life back on the road to life?

2. Consider a social ill that upsets you. Write here the initials of people involved and how you could pray for their transformation by God.

3. It's easy to see John the Baptist as a scolder of people,
but what goals did he hope to accomplish with his
preaching?

What you've been doing to yourself

John diagnoses his congregation's illness as a form of
sloth. They've been "resting in Abraham," expecting their
ancestor's faith to carry them. But salvation isn't in the
genes. They must have suspected this truth themselves. Why
else would they have troubled themselves to trek out from
Jerusalem clear down to the Jordan River? Something must
have been bothering them. Publicly confessing personal sins
wasn't a routine part of their religious expression any more
than it is of ours. Being immersed in the Jordan's muddy
water wasn't their idea of a lark, either. Taking such radical
steps to find forgiveness is usually motivated only by self-
disgust or at least a sense that something is missing, something is askew in one's relationship with God.

John's prescription for these seekers might surprise my
modern-day critics. He doesn't order up a new religion for
them, and he certainly does not whip them into a frenzy to
petition city hall or organize a demonstration against the
religious/civic leaders or undertake a political crusade. Nor
is he content to teach them some new philosophy or to
whisper some mantra they can murmur to find inner peace.

Instead he urges them to repent, to take personal responsibility for their sinfulness, to start life afresh. Neither the
extreme of political activism or of social withdrawal is pre-
scribed. Nothing less than personal renewal will do. John
sets them on the road again, but this time in a new direction

and as newly cleansed persons. As such, they will serve their communities as, in Jesus' words, "the light of the world" and "the salt of the earth." People like this, living a step above the crowd, always conscious of serving others' needs and lifting the downtrodden, can be counted on to take up the burdens of social justice and champion a higher morality. When men and women have experienced repentance and renewal, their society will feel the difference.

A couple of years ago at the invitation of one of the co-teachers, I visited a class jointly sponsored by California State University at Fullerton and Hope International University. Entitled "Judaism, Christianity, and Islam Compared," this upper-division class attracted students from both the state and the Christian universities. Professor Hadad, a Cal State teacher and editor of the Arab Studies Quarterly, was the guest lecturer for that session. Professor Hadad is Syrian Orthodox Christian, but not really by choice, he said. "Most of us are basically what our parents were. If we could go into a tube and be sealed until we were 20, then be put on a chair with representatives from the various religions appearing before us, most of us would choose to be Muslim," he assured the students. "It's the simplest, asks the least (in the way of belief in miracles, extraordinary events). Islam is you and God working out things together."

Professor Hadad's approach intrigued and frustrated me. He treated religion as if it were a commodity to be picked off the shelf, the ingredients quickly scanned, and then selected because it was the best "deal." And the best deal, according to him, was the one requiring the least in the way of belief and obedience.

What do you think? Do you want the simplest and easiest religion—or the truest? Have we comfort-loving Americans reduced religion to this, a casual fling with what does not challenge our minds, summon our energies, or discipline our wills? Have we lost interest in "the way, the truth, and the life" that Jesus promises and that John the Baptist prepares people for?

E. Stanley Jones comes a little closer to the truth than the good professor does. The long-time missionary to India concludes, "there are just two elemental philosophies of life: that of Buddha and that of Christ. The rest are compromises between." They express two diametrically different outlooks on life. Looking at the same facts they came to opposite conclusions, according to Dr. Jones. "One said Yes, and the other No." Gautama Buddha concluded that existence and evil are one. To exist is to be immersed in evil; the way out of evil is out of existence. So the final good is to attain Nirvana, nothingness, the ultimate no.

Jesus, on the other hand, found reason to live, to say yes to life. "I have come that they may have life, and have it to the full" (John 10:10). He is the Great Affirmer, as the apostle Paul asserts in his somewhat enigmatic comments to the Christians in Corinth: "But as surely as God is faithful, our message to you is not 'Yes' and 'No.' For the Son of God, Jesus Christ, who was preached among you by me and Silas and Timothy, was not 'Yes' and 'No,' but in him it has always been 'Yes.' For no matter how many promises God has made, they are 'Yes' in Christ. And so through him the 'Amen' is spoken by us to the glory of God" (2 Corinthians 1:18-20). However, this positive, life-affirming message is apprehended only by those whose faith is in Christ. Jesus put it this way, "You diligently study the Scriptures because you think that by them you possess eternal life. These are the Scriptures that testify about me, yet you refuse to come to me to have life" (John 5:39, 40).

Our refusal to come to Jesus is not so much rebellion, perhaps, as—shall we say it again?—sloth. The deplorable truth is that the way of death is "simpler" than the way of life. John's audience wrongly trusted more in their genetic relationship to Abraham than in their spiritual relationship to God. My well-intentioned critic would have me become a social crusader in order to help people, probably thinking that if I could only do something to create a better social environment then somehow people will be saved. I resist the temptation, even though it is easier to attack social ills than to persuade people to repent and turn back to God, because John has it right and my correspondent has it wrong.

As far as John was concerned, reliance on relatives, on religion—and we could add reliance on some philosophy, or career, or cash, or fame, or social reform, or whatever—does not lead to life. Not only do they fail to solve people's deepest problems, these substitutes for the real thing are sin when taken as replacements for faith in and obedience to God. So, John warns his congregation—and we take heed—you must repent and be baptized.

Tune Up

1. If John the Baptist were to accuse our culture of "sloth," what might he say we've been resting in (as the Jews were resting in Abraham as father, Matthew 3:9)?

2. If we assume that we all should be in the middle of repentance in some way, which of the following phrases describe a repentance you are experiencing now?

  • self-disgust
  • a sense that something is missing
  • sensing that something is amiss in one's relationship with God
  • taking personal responsibility for one's sinfulness
  • starting life afresh

3. What does it say about us when we're interested in a religion that requires little of us?

What I am doing for you

Listen a little more closely to John's sermon. It'll preach today!

• **I'm urging you to repent.** They (we) need a change of mind that leads to a change of attitude that leads to a change of behavior. When we sin and "fall short of the glory of God" (Romans 3:23), we need to take to the road again, but in a different direction, the one that leads to the kingdom of Heaven, where God is sovereign and abundant and eternal life is found by submitting to His will.

• **I'm urging you to produce fruit.** This isn't some kind of salvation by works, the if-I-can-just-work-hard-enough-to-please-God-by-my-good-deeds-I-can-be-saved fruit. To the contrary, John calls specifically for "fruit in keeping with repentance." Are we stretching things too far to jump over to Galatians 5:22, 23 where the apostle Paul specifies the fruit of the Spirit, fruit that certainly looks like it would be the natural product of a life lived in a Godward direction? I don't think so, for "the fruit of the Spirit is love, joy, peace, patience, kindness, goodness, faithfulness, gentleness and self-control." This is the opposite of that produced by "the sinful nature with its passions and desires." It grows in us when "we live by the Spirit, . . . [keeping] in step with the Spirit" (5:25).

• **I'm challenging you to take personal responsibility for your life.** John does not expect his converts to return to Jerusalem the same persons that came to the river to hear him. No more hiding behind Abraham; no mere "faith of our fathers" for them. They can't coast, as unfortunately so many modern church members do, on the hand-me-down religion of their parents or grandparents. Their destiny is in their own hands, and they must grasp it personally.

• **I'm getting you ready to meet your future.** John is the forerunner, the preparer, the announcer who appears on the stage and then, when the star appears, recedes into the wings. He immerses believers in water, cleaning them up so they'll be ready to meet the King. The scrubbing isn't sufficient by itself; John can only remove the surface dirt. The real cleansing, the baptism of Jesus, is yet to come.

On another Sunday registration card, this one written nearly eleven years ago by a man whose growth continues to encourage me, I read: "I feel a little resistance, or maybe a lack of trust toward giving myself to God as I don't want to be disappointed. It's one hell of a threshold to cross. I thought I had [crossed it] through baptism."

Don't be offended by his metaphor. Hell stands for most of us as a symbol for unmitigated suffering, or for supreme disappointment. It's the place of killing and death. For him to trust God completely is a hellish undertaking; something or someone is going to die. He instinctively ties his baptism to this threshold experience. Having died once in baptism, he thought that was enough. It would have been, if the trust, the submission, had been total. It apparently wasn't, and his struggle continues. That was then and this is now. He would not write the same note today, if his fruit-bearing, God-serving life can be taken as evidence of his increased faith.

Do you recall the first registration card note? "Central Christian has turned my life around." I appreciate the sentiment, but it is not quite accurate. Central Christian has played the same role in this young man's life as John the

Baptist played in the lives of those travelers from Jerusalem. His life was turned around, as theirs was, not because of the congregation or the preacher but because of the *One preached.* He crossed the threshold, he turned his life God-ward, he washed away his past in baptism, and is on the road again—but toward a new destiny, toward fruitfulness, toward Heaven. As a responsible human being.

Whatever else we conclude about John's ministry of baptizing, we have to grant its importance. We cannot overlook the climax of this passage (Matthew 3:13-17): Jesus Himself came to be baptized! Bible scholars have debated the significance of this act ever since. Why should Jesus, the sinless one, submit to being baptized by John, who doesn't— because he can't—claim sinlessness? And in what ways does doing so "fulfill all righteousness," as Jesus insists?

We simply don't know more than what Jesus says, except that His act pleases His Father in Heaven. I suspect Jesus was lowered into the Jordan in John's hands to identify with the rest of us. It's the final argument on behalf of baptism. Debate it all you want. At the very least you must admit that Jesus did it and, according to Matthew 28:18-20, He thought we should, too. So we submit to the water and He rewards us with the Spirit. Not a bad bargain.

Tune Up

1. Producing fruit from repentance involves deciding things: wrongs to right; things to do; words to say; prayers to pray. What fruit needs to come out of your repentance?

2. What past achievements, accomplishments, or friend-
ships (if any) have tempted you to "coast" in your relationship with God?

3. If you repent of certain things, how will your future
look different from your past?

4. What sort of character and attitudes are required to live
a life of continual repentance?

What Jesus will do for you

If John's preaching had been primarily a crusade against
people's sins, he might have stirred up an audience but he
could not have been the catalyst for change that he was. He
didn't stop with the obvious. He looked beyond the problem,
even beyond the audience, to the "one who is more powerful
than I, whose sandals I am not fit to carry."

What draws us to John is his humility. He does what he can, and he does it with all his might. But he does not promise what he can't deliver. He is only supporting cast; he doesn't star in the production. He never forgets his role.

• **Jesus will baptize you with the Holy Spirit and with fire.** John can baptize with water, but look what Jesus can do. He will purify, He will inspire, He will guide you.

• **Jesus will judge you.** "His winnowing fork is in his hand." Only He can judge among men and women, discerning wheat from chaff, the Heaven-bound from the Hell-bent.

• **Jesus holds the power to determine your future.** So, John urgently asks, why stay with what isn't working for you (especially since it can't)? Why hang on to a futile faith, a powerless substitute for the real thing?

The way to life is the way of belief in Jesus as Lord and Savior. It is the way of repentance, of turning one's life in a new, Godward direction. This is the message of John the Baptist, of Jesus Himself, and of His church.

But not everyone, certainly not my critic, is impressed with the priority of this message. Nor was eight-year-old Debbie who, after listening to Chuck Swindoll on the radio, asked her six-year-old brother David, "Do you know about Jesus?"

"No," David answered.

His big sister rose to the occasion. "Sit still," she warned David, "cause this is real scary." And her sermon began. After her eight-year-old's explanation, she went right to the Big Question: "Now David, when you die, do you want to go to Heaven to be with Jesus, God, your mommy and daddy and big sister, or do you want to go to the lake of fire to be with the devil and bank robbers?"

David thought a moment, then replied gravely, "I want to stay right here."

Davids of all ages attend my church. They sit impassively as this preacher pours heart and soul into sermon after sermon in the hope that somehow, someday I can get them ready to meet Jesus. But they just want to stay right here. They don't seem to hear the biblical question, "But what if here isn't where you should be?" They are content. They love to hear the preacher "give it" to those other sinners; they applaud when he takes on homosexuals or abortionists or pornographers. But when he talks about their need to repent or their call to help the needy or share the gospel with those outside of Christ, they stare or yawn or check their watches or mentally drift toward more compatible entertainments.

Their inertia makes me recall an old cartoon, just a crudely drawn map. In the upper center section, slightly to the left, an X marks the spot that's labeled, "You are here." But down and over in the lower right-hand corner is another X with a different label: "But should be here." What if here isn't good for them any more, these passive resisters, or at least not good enough? What if in their contentment they are drifting toward disaster? We sympathize with their reluctance to change. Who doesn't hate the confusion, the disorientation, the frightening sensation of dying (on the way to being born again) in the passageway from the familiar to what can be known only through faith?

John speaks to this fear. He is, he says, but a herald announcing the approach of a greater One to come. While they all await His appearing, John gets them ready to meet Him: cleans them with the waters of baptism, teaches them to recognize His appearance, waits with them beside the way. Then Jesus appears. John points to Him as purifier and judge, but also, encouragingly, as the giver of the empowering Holy Spirit. To reverse direction from the wrong way to the right way is tough; it can't ever be easy to admit error, to confess sin, to start over. But if John is right—and the rest of the New Testament corroborates his teaching—Jesus knows how tough it is. That's why He has come to guide us, first personally, then through His Spirit. He is, remember, "The Way."

As one who travels a lot and is often in strange places, I have come to appreciate the magnificence of Jesus' offer. Let me give you one example. I recently ran across an old card that I've been saving since some time back in the 1980s. I was in Masailand in Kenya to visit some missionary friends. As the Land Rover bumped and ground its way over the gravel and dirt road to their home somewhere out in the bush, I held this 3" x 5" card in my hand. There was a note on one side and a hand-drawn map on the other. The note read: "Hi! From Narosura continue on up the hills. At the top when the road turns white go 4 kilometers, turn left, go 4 k to shops at Entesekara. Tim and Marcia Ross live in the last shop on the right. We live 17 k farther on. Pass in front of the shops, on past the front of the school. When you pass under a tree that is falling over the road go just under 1 k and turn R. Follow the tracks to our house. Good luck. Brocks."

"Good luck." I wondered whether that common American expression was quite appropriate coming from missionaries who were preparing to welcome some visiting ministers. "May God guide you," or "the Lord be with you," or some other appeal for God's help seemed more in order as I peered ahead through the seemingly interminable kilometers, hoping that soon the bouncing would stop and the sores and aching would vanish.

Truth to tell, though, I wasn't worried. I held the map, but more importantly, I was not alone. My friend Ted Yamamori was with me. He had been to the Kenya mission field before. Even more significant: our driver was a native Kenyan. He knew every bend in the road, every fallen tree. I had only to trust the One who was The Way.

England's William Temple, commenting on Jesus' famous offer to be "The Way," observed that "it starts where each one stands. We do not have to find its starting place. It starts here where we are."[1]

Which is what John was preaching at the Jordan. "Repent now. Repent here. What you are seeking, the kingdom of

Heaven, is at hand. So the time to start is today; the place to begin is here. The fruit to be produced will start growing immediately."

When you hear this kind of preaching—and take it seriously—you are on the way to life.

Bringing people to life. That was John's calling. And Jesus'. And the church's. And, in case my correspondent is reading this chapter, I must add—mine.

Tune Up

1. What powers and characteristics did Jesus have that John the Baptist did not?

2. In what ways are you being called to die to self (admitting error, confessing sin, and starting over)?

---

[1]Ernest Campbell, *Locked in a Room With Open Doors.* Waco: Word Books, 1974.

CHAPTER 7

THE WAY THROUGH DISLOCATION

Luke 2:1-20

You have known this story since you were a child. You may even have played a role in the Christmas pageant at your church as a somewhat miscast angel, perhaps, or one of the not-quite-in-character shepherds decked out in their dads' bathrobes, valiantly but unsuccessfully trying to stand still while the narrator talked and talked. After all these years, you still savor the words of the *King James Version,* its majestic language eliciting your worship in a way none of the modern versions, more colloquial but lacking the dignity, can. As I said, you are familiar with this story, but it bears revisiting, no matter what time of the year.

This is what my friend Steve Wyatt did a few years ago—and he was surprised at what he found. Steve's a dynamic pastor, a good communicator, and a fine administrator. It was Wyatt the administrator who realized, after a closer look at the text, that if he had been in charge—or "at least a member of the Advent Committee," the whole affair would have run more smoothly. Here is his checklist of the miscues he discovered and would have corrected, if it had been his program:

- Someone forgot to make reservations in Bethlehem— No housing!
- The angelic chorale didn't provide advance notice of their performance—No publicity!

- The Baby's first visitors were smelly shepherds and His first outfit an ugly strip of cloth—No class!
- The bulging mother-to-be was a pregnant teenager—No dignity!
- The delivery room was a stable and those "attending" chewed their cud and whisked flies with their tails—No status!

Things would have been quite different if the ever-efficient Mr. Wyatt had been running them. However, "God didn't ask my opinion," Steve concedes. "So a nondescript virgin in a dilapidated stable delivered to earth—Emmanuel!" And God was with us (that's what Emmanuel means) on His terms.

Steve shared his whimsical aspirations in his church paper. I have no trouble imagining him as one of those mischievous shepherds in Dad's clothes when he was a boy. Now that he's become a man he has put away his childhood acting and has set his sights on directing! He is willing to concede, though, that God knew what He was doing.

Because God was in charge, he adds, "through the Bethlehem event we received

Jesus.
The Christ.
Who shines like the noonday sun.
Whose power makes Niagara seem like a babbling brook.
Whose Word can move galaxies.
Whose mercy covers like a snowstorm.
Whose glory fills the heavens and the earth
like the waters fill the oceans.
Whose love can move the hardest heart."

Jesus. He did it His way. And the world is forever grateful. (Of course, the aspiring director still wants the last word.) "Lord, I've been thinking. . . . About your second coming; I've been jotting down a few ideas. . . ."[1]

Like my friend Steve, I have also been reading the text more closely of late and have discovered a long-overlooked aspect of the story. "'Tis the Season to Be Dislocated" as much as the season to be jolly. When you consider what happened to the key players in the drama, many synonyms of "dislocation" come to mind. People were upset, confused, disordered, disoriented, and moved about by the events swirling around them.

Mary and Joseph, for example. Their dislocation was geographic. Caesar Augustus's order uprooted them from their hometown, Nazareth, and forced them on a laborious journey to Bethlehem. After the birth they were dislocated again, having to camp as refugees in Egypt. And then once again, when it was safe to go back, another difficult trip home.

That census was the periodic head count required by Rome. It formed the tax base that fed the imperial government and provided the data for calling men up for their tours of military duty. The efficient Romans depended on conscripted men to keep the peace, and siphoned levied money to support their luxurious, self-indulgent lifestyle, their magnificent buildings and sporting grounds, and the high costs of administering their far-flung empire. So in answer to Rome's summons, the populace hit the road. Ordered to go home and register, they headed out—and without benefit of planes, trains, and automobiles.

Mary and Joseph were caught in the upheaval, even though she was very near her delivery date. The travails of their travels, though, were nothing compared with the stunning announcements they both heard from angels. This was no ordinary pregnancy. "Mary, you are with child of the Holy Spirit—and your Son will be the savior of the world. You, Mary, innocent and young and hidden away in this nothing of a town, you will become the greatest woman of all human history, but first you'll suffer humiliation and ignominy because nobody's going to believe what I'm telling you—that the child is from God and not from a man."

"Joseph, don't be afraid to marry Mary. She's not been promiscuous. It's because she has been so faithful to God that she was selected to bear the child that is not yours but will be yours to raise as you will your other children. Yours is the supportive role in this drama. You will provide for the child and His mother, you will keep them out of harm's way, you will devote yourself to them now and you will bear the stigma of the neighbors' gossip. Your life will never be the same, Joseph. But don't be afraid."

Tune Up

1. Why do you suppose God allowed the advent of the Christ to be so disorderly?

2. How easy is it for you to see God working in interruptions and dislocations?
   ❑ easy
   ❑ not so easy
   ❑ very difficult

3. Reread this last paragraph of paraphrased instructions to Joseph. If you had been Joseph, what might have been your first response before you came around and did exactly what you were told?

The shepherds' sense of confusion must have been nearly overwhelming. Were they hallucinating? They were men of the fields. They knew the lay of the land; they had memorized the positions of the stars in the night and kept their calendars by the shape of the moon. But they had never seen such sights in the sky or heard such sounds in the firmament. When the angel had spoken and the hosts of angels had left them and they realized they hadn't been fantasizing, they did what they had to do. They rushed to the birthplace; they worshiped the Christ child. Then they told everyone who would listen to their report.

But what happened to them later? Surely they were never the same again. You can hear them telling their story, year after year, until reaching old age, their listeners are worn out with the hearing of it, saying to each, "Yes, yes, old man, we've heard your tale and we believe that you believe it happened. You saw something wonderful. It changed you forever. So you say. So you believe. But what's that to us? That was long ago and far away and we have to get on now with life. The angels haven't said a word to me." Do you think the shepherds ever felt completely at home again among their doubting, even patronizing, families and neighbors? They were no longer your common, run-of-the-mill shepherds. They had seen the glory, and it changed them forever.

The innkeeper just puts in a cameo appearance. He speaks to the weary couple for a moment, protests he has no room, then relents and lets Mary and Joseph bed down with the stable animals. At least that's our guess. Actually, he doesn't really appear. The text says Jesus was born in a manger "because there was no room for them in the inn." No more details. We have to make up the scene. No matter how we stage it, the innkeeper's role is in a way the most pathetic of all the characters. He may never have realized who his surprise guests were. That he took pity on the very pregnant young woman is probably an accurate guess; why else would he have bothered? Joseph would not have elicited such sympathy on his own; with the town crowded with outsiders, let the man fend for himself. He can sleep in the fields. But the woman, so obviously in discomfort, ah, for her something must be done.

Have you ever wondered whether the unusual goings on out back made any impression on the innkeeper? Did he even notice? Shepherds were a pretty common sight in town, after all, picking up supplies, bargaining for the best deal, mingling with the hordes of visitors. I don't know. Would he have had time to visit the stable himself, to check on the little family, to offer a cover against the night chill? Those swaddling cloths —did they come from the inn? You hope, don't you, that on this most momentous of all occasions the harried host would have taken notice. But it's pretty difficult even for God to make a difference to busy people—and this man was busy. Was his dislocation just a moment on a crowded evening?

Luke doesn't tell us about **the wise men**. We learn of them in Matthew's version of the Christmas story. The first Gospel provides very little information about them, but it's all we have. Were they astrologers? Court advisers? Learned scholars? All of the above? T. S. Eliot recounts their journey in one of his greatest poems, "The Journey of the Magi." According to one of the wise men, reminiscing in his old age, it was a most difficult journey. "A hard time we had of it," bearing with bad weather, unfriendly towns, and the curses of their cantankerous camel men. A hard time.

Then they arrived, finding the Christ child "not a moment too soon." The old man doesn't speak of celebration or revelation or even surprise. The event, "was (you may say) satisfactory." That's it. Nothing earthshaking or life changing, at least at the time.

"But set down / This set down," he urges the poem's reader. Although the experience seemed rather commonplace at the time, after pondering it for many years he realizes it has transformed his life. He and his companions took the hard journey because of a birth. Now he wonders whether it was for a birth or a death. He has come to understand that Christ's birth means his own death. The man he was before meeting Jesus has died. He can't even feel at home in his own country. His countrymen have become "an alien people clutching their gods." Having met Jesus, he is alienated from his own people. Their culture, their values, their busy-ness about so many unimportant things has made them like strangers to him. He can't be like them any longer. But do not think he resents the change. "I should be glad of another death," he concludes. Dislocated, disoriented—and then re-oriented to a newer, better way of life.

We don't like to talk about **King Herod**, the arch-villain of the story. His "dislocation" wasn't geographic, but Jesus' birth caused no one to become more upset than this stinking-from-sickness monster of a monarch. He appears on the Bible's pages as the personification of evil. A very old man when Jesus was born, Herod was ravaged by illness (some think it was syphilis) and nearly eaten up with paranoia. He would (and did) kill anybody, even his own wife, who seemed to his demented mind to threaten his throne. So when the wise men innocently inquired in Jerusalem pre-cisely where the new king—that this was a royal birth they had surmised from their astrological charts—was to be born, the wily sovereign insinuated himself into their confidence and, having learned from his own counselors that the Christ was to be born in Bethlehem, sent them on their way with his blessing. He asked only that they report their findings to him, "so that I too may go and worship him" (Matthew 2:8).

Worship was the last thing on his agenda, of course. When they eluded his grasp by returning to the East via another route, Herod showed his true colors. He did what evil men always do. They destroy whatever gets in their way. He ordered the killing of "all the boys in Bethlehem and its vicinity who were two years old and under." For the inno-cents and their families, Christmas spelled tragedy. And Herod? He earned his perpetual place in history. Without the dislocation of the birth event, this otherwise mediocre king in a remote outpost of the Roman Empire would have been consigned to oblivion somewhere in the ancient past.

⚌ Tune Up ⚌

1. How do you think seeing the angels that night would
   have changed the shepherds forever?

2. When was the last time you met someone in a dislocated state of mind (this might even be a newcomer at
   church) and did some small unusual thing to help him
   or her (as the innkeeper did)?

3. How do you explain the fact that God cosmically
   invited pagan soothsayers to worship Jesus?

   This closer look at the disrupting effect of Jesus' birth
isn't painted on our Christmas cards. We prefer New England snow scenes, the horse-drawn sleigh approaching the
old homestead, flames dancing in the fireplace, smoke curl-
ing through the cold night air, freshly driven snow covering
everything in a blanket of innocence. We dream of our white
Christmases, of tearing into our packages beside the tree, of
relatives coming and going, of the white clapboard church

nestled amid the firs, music from the choir wafting over the stilled countryside. Christmas symbolizes continuity, stability, safety.

For some of us the truth is quite otherwise, much more like the upsetting experiences of the Advent characters. Christmas fractures our normal habits. For a few days in December the routine is frustrated. We force time into the schedule for shopping and partying, dash off on a trip to Grandma's, make ourselves be nice to the relatives, even join the rest of them at church for a special worship service. In the Yule season things get turned upside down. We feel somehow dislocated, but we cope.

For others, Christmas is the most depressing season of the year. Prisoners, military personnel, the hospitalized, the separated, the divorced, the never-married, the bereaved, the homeless—for them, 'tis not "the season to be jolly." The celebration of Jesus' birth is not the cause of their sense of dislocation; they really *are* out of place, where they don't belong, surrounded by the season's intruding reminders of their alienation. Your "Merry Christmas" is their "Bah, Humbug!"

And yet—we can't give them the last word. There are too many others who share their dislocation but not their misery. We hear from them every year—from their prisons, military posts, hospitals, apartments, even their temporary shelters and from the depths of their bereavement or separation.

They have not neglected the most important person in the story. They identify with Him. The babe in the manger, for whom there was no room; the refugee in Egypt with a price on His head; the poor itinerant teacher who had no place to call His own; the convicted criminal who committed no crime; the assassinated holy man whose good deeds incited evil men to murder; the lonely teacher whose closest friends did Him in. All who identify with Jesus cannot give in to self-pity when they locate God's love for them in His cross. They are grateful for His sacrifice.

Tune Up

1. How can knowing Christ help a person go through dislocation, interruptions, and even chaos without misery?

2. Which of the descriptions of Christ in the last paragraph do you find most jarring?

That sacrifice bears revisiting. Say the word and we automatically think of the cross, of the price He paid for our salvation. The crucifixion stands for most Christians as the ultimate expression of God's love for sinners like us. Christmas is for singing, for merriment; Good Friday, on the other hand, we set aside to remember His death. No sugar plums, no dancing, no chestnuts roasting on an open fire. We don't deck the halls with boughs of holly; we drape the cross in black. And we give thanks for His sacrifice.

We have it all backwards. Jesus' death was not His greatest sacrifice. His birth was. When we partake of Communion, we properly thank God for the gift of Jesus' life, taken from Him on that cross. But in truth, His best gift was in coming from His home to ours, from the timeless radiance of His Father's presence to the pain and grime of ours.

As the Bible puts it, .

He is the image of the invisible God, the firstborn over all creation. For by him all things were created: things in heaven and on earth, visible and invisible, whether thrones or powers or rulers or authorities; all things were created by him and for him.   Colossians 1:15, 16

In the beginning was the Word, and the Word was with God, and the Word was God. He was with God in the beginning. Through him all things were made; without him nothing was made that has been made. In him was life, and that life was the light of men.   John 1:1-4

Bible writers reach to the edges of their vocabulary to express the inexpressible; that the eternal, invisible, creative, life-giving and life-defining sustainer of all reality would leave His "location" to join us. Paul praises this one "Who, being in very nature God, did not consider equality with God something to be grasped, but made himself nothing, taking the very nature of a servant, being made in human likeness" (Philippians 2:6).

Thus Madeleine L'Engle, writing nearly two millennia later, imagines Mary musing on the meaning of her son's relocation to earth. Trying to grasp the immense distance Jesus traveled from equality with God to identity with us humans, she pictures herself being born as "one of the small wood lice / in the doorsill of our house." What would it be like to cram herself into something so small, so un-human-like, that she could be comprehended by one "of those small dark creatures, / unable to know sea or sun or song?" Even that restricted existence, she realizes, "would be as nothing, nothing to the radiant Word / coming to dwell" in man's "confined and cabined flesh."[2]

Jesus' birth was for Him then, as it is for us now, a dislocating event, upsetting the routine, dislodging us from our comfort, forcing unwelcome change. The birthing occurred in the area of Bethlehem. Even that simple fact underscores God's flair for the unexpected. The distance from Jerusalem to Bethlehem is not very far, at best about five miles. Yet what a difference those miles make. You'd expect anything as consequential as this divine birth would have to happen in the capital city, Jerusalem, the holy city, not in little Bethlehem, where no one (Micah excepted) ever expected anything this important to happen. It's not that kind of town. Quiet, unchanging, undramatic Bethlehem now stands in our imagination not so much as a location as the place of dislocation —for the parents, the shepherds, the innkeeper, the wise men, the king—and the King.

And yet, and yet. Bethlehem paradoxically has become the location of significance for the formerly disconnected, the displaced person, the stranger. Remember the Christmas pageant? Why are children still reenacting the drama after so many years? Isn't it because of the warmth of the stable, the hospitality of the holy family in welcoming the shepherds, and the satisfaction found by those strangers from the East? Doesn't it help them become relocated—in relation to God, to other humans, to loved ones?

Years ago our family was among the dislocated. I had uprooted the four of us (Mom, Dad, and two children under two years old) from our security in Oregon and moved us across the continent to East Tennessee. There we faced our first Christmas away from our families and loved ones. To stave off the loneliness, we did what Christian families have always done—we sought out other believers with whom to spend the holidays. We "borrowed" some special new friends as grandparents for our little ones. They've remained treasured friends to this day. We repeated this practice in Indiana a few years later, and then in Arizona still later. In each new locality we now have irreplaceable friends through whose love we learned that relocated people don't have to feel dislocated—when their shared locus is the Babe of Bethlehem.

It was relatively easy for us to make the adjustments because everywhere we moved there was a welcoming church. We have been spared the agony of many who are reminded at Christmas that they have not "located" a place of their own. I mentioned them above: prisoners, service personnel on assignment, the hospitalized, the residents of rest homes, diplomats, professional men and women, and many others in this mobile generation who dream of Christmas, white or otherwise, lamenting the lack of a home for the holidays. And the other days.

Dislocated. Away from home. Upset. Needing to get to Bethlehem. Steve Wyatt's final insight is the right one: God knew what He was doing. He arranged for the birth where it was not expected. He meant to startle Mary and Joseph, to astonish the shepherds, to exasperate Herod, to lure the wise men from the East, and to keep on causing men and women everywhere to be upset—literally—by the life-changing touch of the Son. He could see that we would revisit Bethlehem every Christmas, even more faithfully than we go to Grandma's. The stable, the manger, the shepherds, and the wise men—they form a single scene. They've become a kind of touchstone for us. In our wanderings, through all our dislocations and confusions and disorientations—yes, in our lostness—we remember that if we can just get back to Bethlehem, to the manger, to the One whose drastic change of environment must have been the ultimate culture shock, who is the true locus of our lives, if we can just get to Him we can find our way home, back to God, back to sanity, back to life.

I am the way and the truth and the life.   John 14:6

Tune Up

1. What does Jesus' gift of coming from His home to ours, from the timeless radiance of His Father's presence to the pain and grime of ours, tell us about the heart of Christ?

2. Go back to the quotation of Colossians 1:15, 16. Picture Christ as a baby. Read it aloud and then picture Christ as a baby again. What does this make you want to say to Christ?

3. In retrospect, how has God worked in your life in a dislocating event that upset your routine, dislodged you from comfort, and forced unwelcome change?

4. How is God calling you to come alongside a "dislocated" person and perhaps entertain "angels unawares" (Hebrews 13:2, KJV)?

---

[1]"Straight from Steve," *Cullen Ave News,* December 4, 1995.

[2]We have sought to secure permissions for all copyrighted material in this book, but were unable to document this quote. The publisher expresses regret.

THE WAY BACK FROM THE WRONG ROAD

Acts 9:1-22

Some people have a gift for taking the wrong road. I sometimes wonder whether I'm one of them. More than one of our family vacation trips could be summarized: "Mostly we turned around and went back." I have a fairly good sense of direction and after several miles a growing uneasiness will take over and, usually with some word of explanation to my wife as to how, through no fault of my own, we seem to have taken the wrong road back there—or, even better, that I had in fact intended to check out this fascinating part of the country but now it's time to get back on the main road—we'll retrace our journey. Unfortunately, when the sky is overcast or the night is black, as it was recently when one of our adult kids and I were trying to join the rest of the family at a remote Oregon lake, my directional abilities abandon me and I'm at the mercy of any locals I can find—and there are precious few to find at 11:30 P.M. in the unpopulated Central Oregon mountains. (Fortunately—or probably more accurately I should say providentially—we found one whose knowledge was sure and whose spirit was helpful.)

Getting lost is a pretty common human experience. Anybody who has traveled almost anywhere can liven up a party with a, "Let me tell you about the time I got really lost" story. When you are safely home, your "lost" stories provide good entertainment.

But what if you aren't safely home? What if you're still on the wrong road, headed in the wrong direction? Then nobody's laughing.

You undoubtedly are already familiar with the story of Saul of Tarsus, the brilliant, ambitious, some would say fanatical religious leader whose passion was to wipe out the growing sect of Jesus followers. We could quarrel with his tactics, but not with his motivation. His ambition was to please God. He gave everything he had to earn God's favor. He later described himself as "a Hebrew of Hebrews; in regard to the law, a Pharisee; as for zeal, persecuting the church; as for legalistic righteousness, faultless" (Philippians 3:5, 6). A good, a righteous man. But a man on the wrong road. "Breathing out murderous threats against the Lord's disciples," he stalked them. The heresy had to be stamped out. A good man, a zealous man, he could not rest as long as anyone was in danger of converting to Jesus.

Had you warned him he was on the wrong road, he'd have scoffed at you. He was serving God!

If he had kept going, we would never have heard of this man. Acts 9 tells his story. We still study it today, because his turnaround has pointed the way for generations of believers ever since.

The first lesson we learn from him is this one:

You won't find your way back until you admit you're on the wrong road.

In the Bible, this turnaround is called *repentance,* which is simply a change of mind that leads to a change of behavior. It's more than remorse, which readily says, "I'm sorry," as Saul (whom we know as the apostle Paul) later admits. Remorse is what he calls "worldly sorrow," and that "brings death" (2 Corinthians 7:10). Not so with "godly sorrow." Its fruit is the "repentance that leads to salvation and leaves no regret." The real thing isn't satisfied with mumbling a few words of apology. To the contrary. It's the beginning of another journey, on a road leading in a new direction, toward a sure destination and a satisfied soul.

Tune Up

1. Underline words in the text above that could be used to define repentance.

2. Imagine for a moment a person caught in adultery. In the right column, write an example of this person showing remorse (top row) and repentance (bottom row)

2 Corinthians 7:10

Remorse; worldly sorrow; brings death

Repentance; godly sorrow; leads to salvation, leaves no regret

Repentance looks a lot like humility. In Saul's case, the transformation from self-assured persecutor to obedient follower is dramatic. After Jesus confronts him on the road to Damascus, the intense, driven, fire-breathing oppressor can't even find his way without help. When we next see him in Ananias's home, he's blind, helpless—and tame, passively accepting succor from the very people he had sought to harm. Saul the Hunter had become Saul the Captured. Saul was smart enough to know he was beaten. When he learned, to his amazement, that the Jesus whose influence he was trying to stamp out was the Lord Himself, he capitulated immediately. "Immediately" is Luke's word, not mine.

May I pause for a moment over the role of sorrow in repentance? Back in 1998 President Bill Clinton, after leading the country through an agonizing eight months of insistent denials that he had sexual relations with Monica Lewinsky, was at long last trapped into making some kind of statement. In carefully crafted sentences he admitted to inappropriate behavior, insisted on his right to have a private life, attacked the prosecuting attorney Kenneth Starr, and in general left the American populace wondering whether *this time* he was telling the truth. Not until Mr. Starr delivered the incriminating evidence to Congress did Mr. Clinton come full circle and say, with apparent sincerity, that he was sorry for what he had done wrong, sorry for hurting his friends, family, the American people, and Miss Lewinsky and her family.

But his agony wasn't over yet. He had said the words. What his fellow citizens wanted to know and waited to see was whether he meant what he said—or was it just another performance?

That's the difference that repentance makes. The difference is found in the fruit it bears. You can't distinguish remorse from repentance by the words spoken, only by the life lived. Once you have claimed to repent, you can't return to business as usual. John the Baptist preached this sermon before Jesus did: "Produce fruit in keeping with repentance." With his saltiest vocabulary he thundered at the crowds (who came to hear a good sermon and maybe to be baptized), "You brood of vipers! Who warned you to flee from the coming wrath?" He would not baptize them (as a demonstration of their repentance) if they had any intention of returning to their reptilian ways. They must prove their sorrow; they must get off the wrong road and head out on the one leading to a productive, God-led life. Saying "I'm sorry" wouldn't—and won't—cut it.

Back in the mid '80s a fine conference on biblical exposition was held in California. This preacher really wanted to attend, but my schedule prevented it, so Chris Sewell, a British intern on our staff that year, went in my place. He came back with a bundle of notes, making me regret my absence even more. Among the best stories he relayed to me was one that Chuck Colson told about a man who was traveling on an airline. He was hungry, so he was more than ready when his lunch pack was delivered. His anticipation quickly turned to disgust, though, when he spied a roach sitting just under the plastic film. He was so upset he determined to write to the company when he returned, which he did in the strongest terms he could employ. He didn't really expect a reply, so he was quite surprised to receive a letter of regret from the airline a week later. The letter went like this:

Dear Sir: We want to express our deepest regret at your recent experience while traveling on our airline. We want you to know that we have taken every step possible to see that it will never happen again. We have taken that aircraft out of service, stripped the interior and had it fumigated. The caterers have been replaced and we have fired the member of the staff who was on duty and responsible for serving you with that meal.

We have done everything in our power to rectify the situation and we can assure you that this will NEVER happen again. We do hope that you can see how much we value your patronage and we hope that you will fly with us again.

Yours sincerely, . . . President

The man was duly impressed. He wondered whether perhaps he had overreacted. This airline really cared. Then he noticed another piece of paper in the envelope and discovered that a careless secretary had accidentally put his letter into the envelope with the reply. He opened it up and idly reread it. Then turned it over. On back was a hastily scribbled note: "Send the standard roach letter."

So much for saying "I'm sorry." In faith as in love, talk is cheap. Faith without deeds is dead. Jesus said it best, "By their fruit you will recognize them."

There is no doubt that Saul's repentance was real. He turned around "cold turkey." He not only stopped persecuting Christians, he joined them.

Applying this principle more broadly, Jay Carty suggests a solution for overcoming habits that drive us down ("down" is an instructive word here, isn't it?) the wrong road. Again, admitting you're sorry for your addiction to alcohol or drugs or pornography, or whatever, is not enough. Carty's advice is direct: "Figure out where you lose control and then back up one step. If it's hard for you to drive by that adult book store, drive home another route; if soaps send you into sexual fantasy, don't turn on the TV—unplug it, watch CNN or ESPN, or put your foot through the screen."[1] In other words, get off the wrong road. You need another route, one that leads up, not down, toward God, not toward destruction.

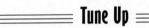

Tune Up

1. How does repentance require humility?

2. Consider something for which you have repented. If repentance is measured not by words spoken, but by the life lived, is your repentance still intact? Why or why not?

3. What does the airline letter story tell us about the ways we fake repentance?

4. In what matter could you follow the practical advice, "figure out where you lose control and then back up one step"?

Being on the wrong road isn't a sign that you're a bad person.

This must be said. Whenever a preacher approaches the subject of repentance, he loses people in the audience who can protest, with some justification, "But I'm not a bad person." And they're right. That could have been Saul's protest. In fact, as we've already noted, according to everything Saul knew about righteousness, he was one of the best. Remember his self-description: "as for legalistic righteousness, faultless."

Repentance isn't a prescription only for bad people. As in Saul's case, it is the right medicine for good people as well. These well-intentioned souls always mean to do good, live right, do their duties, love their families, serve their country. By their limited lights, they're the best. They just don't see things as God does—that's why they need to turn around. They don't have the right perspective. It's their direction that is wrong, not their character.

Good as they are, they're still headed for trouble. C. S. Lewis helpfully points out that the language in the Old

Prayer Book, that we are "miserable offenders," isn't describing our feelings but is using an older meaning of miserable—that we are objects of pity. We may feel fine about ourselves, but in spite of our good feelings our situation is still pitiful. Lewis's example is to imagine that we are looking down from a high vantage point on two crowded express trains. We can see that they are speeding towards one another on the same track, both trains moving at sixty miles an hour. Their deplorable state is certain, though the passengers are feeling fine. Their satisfaction doesn't change the fact that their condition is miserable.[2]

Saul felt fine about himself and his mission. He was a "miserable offender" who didn't feel miserable; he wasn't aware of any offense against God. "Who are you, Lord?" The innocence of his question is all the more poignant when compared with his later knowledge of God. A misdirected career. Numbers of Christians mistakenly persecuted. Incredible damage inflicted. By a man who felt totally justified.

That's how he felt. No matter. He was still guilty.

A friend of mine walked out on his wife. This sad story is made all the sadder because my friend was a minister with an outstanding career. His churches rapidly increased in membership, his reputation grew even more rapidly. When he left her, his appraisal of himself and the situation was stunning. He was on top of the world. About himself and his decision, he said he felt just fine, thank you.

His wife of many years had a different opinion. She feared for his future. He had mounted his charger and was galloping toward destruction. You would have had a hard time convincing her that her self-confident (nay, let's say it— self-righteous) husband wasn't really a miserable offender.

She believed, as does this writer, that the Psalms speak an inviolable truth:

> The sacrifices of God are a broken spirit;
>> a broken and contrite heart,
>> O God, you will not despise.   Psalm 51:17

The spirit of brokenness is the proper attitude toward God —not just for bad people, but for anyone traveling the wrong road.

To get on the right road you don't have to become who you aren't.

We've all heard so many stories of dramatic conversions, of lives radically turned around, that it would be easy to misunderstand repentance. Genuine repentance isn't about changing who you are. You undoubtedly need to change some attitudes and even some behavior (Saul had to quit picking on the Christians), but God isn't interested in changing the basic you. He created you, after all. He values you. He just wants you on the right road.

Think of Saul again. Even as he was hounding the saints, he was displaying his incredible combination of talents. Once he got on the right road, employing his abilities as God, rather than he, willed, he proved to be an unstoppable dynamo in Christ's service. Consider just some of his assets: abundant energy, enthusiasm, intensity, intelligence, fearlessness, leadership, wide learning, teachability, compassion, spiritual sensitivity, perseverance, deep faith, unquenchable hope, flexibility, adaptability, articulateness—the list goes on and on. None of these did Saul have to scuttle on his way to becoming the apostle Paul.

Tune Up

1. At what moments do we especially need to be reminded that repentance isn't just for bad people, but is the "right medicine for good people as well"?

2. What does it take to be a person who continually heads in the right direction, day after day?

3. If God were to change your direction (yet still use your helpful traits and strong points), in what direction might you be headed?

———————————————————
———————————————————

Paul did have to change his mind and reform some attitudes. He would later urge other disciples not to "conform any longer to the pattern of this world, but be transformed by the renewing of your mind" (Romans 12:2). Paul's word "transformed" is *metamorphous,* from which we get the English "metamorphosis." Your mind changes, not in ability, but in focus and value system. Repentance, the word I've been employing in this chapter to describe the turning around from the wrong road and taking the right one, is the Greek *metanoia.* A good translation is "reformation," being re-formed, made like new —starting over, going back to the fork in the road and taking the right one this time.

But you don't have to become somebody else. God doesn't want who you aren't but who you are, thinking God's thoughts after Him, choosing to do His will.

Let me offer an example from a different sphere. During America's civil rights war, no politician yelled his way into more headlines than Alabama's Governor George Wallace, who has been called "the most influential loser in modern American politics." Four times he ran for the Presidency without getting to move into the White House. He served four terms as Alabama's governor. In 1968 he played the spoiler, so dividing the Democratic Party that he caused Hubert Humphrey to lose to Richard Nixon. He ran again in 1972, but this time a would-be assassin's bullet left him permanently crippled. It was, in a sense, his Damascus Road experience. Wheelchair-bound, he was forced to think more deeply, to face himself more honestly than ever before. He saw the consequences of his reckless rhetoric and racist tactics. He had thought of himself as the champion of the poor and helpless, but he had not included African-Americans in his concern. His racist epithets were headlined across the nation.

Late in 1978 he appeared unannounced at the Dexter Avenue Baptist Church in Montgomery (Martin Luther King, Jr.'s church). Three hundred black ministers and lay leaders of Alabama churches were concluding a day-long conference. The governor, who thought he would be leaving office for the last time shortly, was wheeled into the building and up to the foot of the pulpit. Then he told the ministers, "I never had hate in my heart for any person. But I regret my support of segregation and the pain it caused the black people of our state and nation." Then he added, "I've learned what pain is and I'm sorry if I've caused anybody else pain. Segregation was wrong—and I am sorry."[3]

His later years in office offered proof that he meant what he said. In the end he earned the respect of the people he had formerly attacked. He will be remembered as a governor who labored hard for the welfare of all his people, including African-Americans. By his fruit he proved his repentance.

So did Saul.

Finding the road back usually involves an Ananias.

The metamorphosis of Saul of Tarsus into the apostle
Paul was advanced through the good offices of Ananias.
Forgiver, receiver, reconciler, conduit of God's grace—
that's Ananias. Reluctant at first—and not without cause;
Saul had a reputation, remember—Ananias conquered his
fear. No more powerful words are spoken in Scripture than
these two: "Brother Saul. . . ." Brother Saul! What grace
Ananias packs into his greeting. What depth of unexpressed
feeling, what stifled confusion about God's purposes. With
simple obedience and complete trust, Ananias sweeps away
Saul's past and welcomes him into God's gracious present.

Repentance does not always involve an intermediary. We
think, for example, of the prodigal son in Jesus' famous
parable who on his own came to his senses: "I will set out
and go back to my father" (Luke 15:18). His situation was
deplorable; good Jewish boys didn't slop hogs. Something
had to be done—and he did it. No Ananias needed.

Sometimes the catalytic agent is a kind of anti-Ananias,
one whose non-forgiving, very judgmental spirit forces the
sinner to introspection and disgust. John DeLorean offers a
good example. (Do you remember his ill-fated DeLorean
automobile?) This one-time darling of the automotive world
suddenly found himself in court, accused of dealing drugs.
In the fight of his life, he hoped to salvage what was left of
his empire. The pivotal moment for him came during a key
government witness's testimony. DeLorean knew him to be
a paid informer, and as the witness piled lie upon lie and
reported conversations that had never taken place, DeLorean
was wracked with questions: *Why is he doing this? To what
end is he building this totally false story?* In the midst of his
anger and frustration, though, came what he called an
epiphany. He saw in the witness a mirror image of his own
life. "I had a moment of *deja vu*. I came face to face with
the old John DeLorean in all his prideful pursuit of fame,
power, and glory." This man's ambitious lying was no

different from his own blind drive for power and success, DeLorean concluded. Both men had been trampling on whoever got underfoot. Humbled, he sought God's forgiveness.[4]

For most of us, though, there's an Ananias in our story, a wise counselor, an accepting, brave, and forgiving Christian who risked misunderstanding and rejection to reach out to our lostness and, with love and modesty, refusing to be intimidated by our past or even our present condition, grasped our hand in his (or, perhaps more often, hers) and uttered an embracing, "Brother . . ." or "Sister. . . ."

There must be a special place in Heaven for the Ananiases of this world.

The right road doesn't promise to be any easier than the wrong one.

A disconcerting note is introduced to the account. "This man is my chosen instrument to carry my name before the Gentiles and their kings and before the people of Israel. *I will show him how much he must suffer for my name.*" Sorry. This chapter doesn't teach a "Name It and Claim It" gospel. Instead it points to an inescapable fact: Life is about suffering. God does not promise Saul that from here on out, now that he is on the right road, his troubles are over.

Saul already knew what we pampered Americans have difficulty accepting, that whether you are religious or irreligious, wealthy or impoverished, intelligent or otherwise, even lucky or hapless, life involves suffering. Period. If you care, if you love, if you believe, if you follow Jesus, your life will include distress, loss, misunderstanding, even persecution. And if you don't do any of the above, you will suffer anyway.

Since pain is inescapable, you might as well suffer for what matters, not what doesn't. This was the conclusion of a visitor to Mozambique, which has been plagued by fighting and the famines of incessant warfare. He reported that the loudest complaining he heard there, the most emotional voices, were not raised as you would expect in the famine-ravaged countryside, but in the capital city, Maputo, which was spared the worst of the war. There, he said, "great bellows of rage and grief often woke me in the mornings." The sufferers were the same every day. They were South African and Portuguese businessmen who were playing tennis on the courts below his hotel window. Suffering—over a tennis game.

The apostle Paul learned well the lesson of which God spoke to Ananias. In 2 Corinthians 11:24-29 he recounts what he has been through.

> Five times I received from the Jews the forty lashes minus one. Three times I was beaten with rods, once I was stoned, three times I was shipwrecked, I spent a night and a day in the open sea, I have been constantly on the move. I have been in danger from rivers, in danger from bandits, in danger from my own countrymen, in danger from Gentiles; in danger in the city, in danger in the country, in danger at sea; and in danger from false brothers. I have labored and toiled and have often gone without sleep; I have known hunger and thirst and have often gone without food; I have been cold and naked. Besides everything else, I face daily the pressure of my concern for all the churches. Who is weak, and I do not feel weak? Who is led into sin, and I do not inwardly burn?

Repentance—not a guarantee of a smooth journey but a take-off in the right direction.

God knows where you are even when you don't.

We've come to the end of the study. Over the whole chapter—the whole book, for that matter—is the hovering presence of God, biding His time, waiting for our readiness—or arranging it.

Try as we might, there's no escape from God. We refer to

the sovereignty of God for a reason. He is in charge, wherever we are. If we'll just look in the right places, we can see evidence of His presence. David is not the only sinner who has asked,

> Where can I go from your Spirit?
> Where can I flee from your presence?
> If I go up to the heavens, you are there;
>   if I make my bed in the depths, you are there.
> If I rise on the wings of the dawn,
>   if I settle on the far side of the sea,
> even there your hand will guide me,
>   your right hand will hold me fast.
>
> Psalm 139:7-10

That being the case, it is the better part of wisdom, isn't it, to come to the same position that David adopted?

> Search me, O God, and know my heart;
>   test me and know my anxious thoughts.
> See if there is any offensive way in me,
>   and lead me in the way everlasting.
>
> Psalm 139:23, 24

It's the right way.

Tune Up

1. Who has been an "Ananias" in your life (a Christian who has reached out to your lostness, perhaps risking misunderstanding and rejection)?

2. Is there someone God is calling you to be an Ananias to just now?

3. Have you been hesitant to follow a new direction because it might involve suffering of some kind? Whether you answer "yes" or "no," reread the verses above from Psalm 139. Underline a phrase or two that would be helpful if someday your answer would be "yes."

---

[1]Jay Carty, *Counterattack.* Portland, Oregon: Multnomah Press, 1988.

[2]*The Business of Heaven,* ed. Walter Hooper. Great Britain: Fount Paperbacks, 1984.

[3]Stephan Lesher, "The Tangled Legacy of George Wallace," *The Wall Street Journal,* August 24, 1994.

[4]Ravi Zacharias, *Can Man Live Without God?* Dallas, et al: Word Publishing, 1994.

CHAPTER 9

THE WAY OF FORGIVENESS

Philemon 8-22

The thesis of this chapter is very simple: If you want to enjoy long-lasting relationships, you have to learn to forgive. Period.

You can argue all you want about who is at fault and how much you've been injured and that you are "more sinned against than sinning," and you may win all your arguments —and remain very lonely.

There is no better source to help us understand forgiveness than Paul's letter to his fellow Christian Philemon. If you didn't understand before reading the brief epistle you will by the time you've finished: the Christian faith is about relationships, and relationships demonstrate love, and love forgives. That's it.

I'm writing this chapter with a heavy heart. As I have confessed elsewhere, my family is riddled with divorce. My parents were married nineteen years before they went their separate ways. Both my sister and my brother live alone after being married and divorced. One daughter has been divorced, the other married a man who had been divorced. Of our "adopted" children, all are from divorced homes. Only Joy and I have remained married and, I always must add, that is to Joy's credit and not mine.

My heart is heavy because of the most recent—and unnecessary—divorce in the family. Both partners contributed to the marriage's demise; neither could claim innocence. But the precipitating cause was a young man's inability to forgive. As a result, he lost his wife, has cut off his sister, and has walked away from a family that loves him. He insists he did no wrong (in fact, that he has never done wrong), that he can never forgive, and that whatever has happened to estrange him from so many people is all their fault.

On the other hand, there is cause for rejoicing in our family. Jeff, one of our adopted sons, who has been "ours" for over thirty-five years, has so appreciated his special place in our family that he has carried on the tradition, claiming two unofficially adopted sons of his own. And one of those, a young man we'll call Jim, in turn took another younger man (we'll name him John) under his wing. But that relationship hit a snag.

I don't know what caused the breach in their relationship, but when Jim was relating the problem to his "dad," Jeff, he explained that he had pulled away from John. The problem was too serious for Jim to tolerate, he said. Jeff paused a moment, considered, then quietly said to Jim, "I can't imagine doing anything that would make Roy have nothing to do with me." When Jeff recounted the incident to me, I had difficulty speaking for a moment, first, because I was moved that Jeff understood how completely I love him, and secondly, because of Jeff's insight into the meaning of that love. Jeff is a remarkable man in many ways and I'm very proud of him. But like his adoptive father, he isn't perfect. He knows that, and so do I. But it isn't his perfection that I want; it's the relationship with him that I cherish. And that relationship isn't possible without our mutual forgiveness.

In a recent conversation with a distraught wife, the same issue emerged. She was convinced her husband had been unfaithful. She didn't accuse him of having a physical affair with another woman, but what was equally despicable to her, an emotional one that had left her feeling betrayed, misunderstood, and very resentful. Then to add to her anger, when she insisted that they receive counseling, he refused. She was as frustrated, she said, as she had ever been in her life. She was convinced that they could never get beyond their current impasse without the help of a counselor.

As I listened to her, however, I wasn't convinced. Counseling is often very helpful. Having been a pastoral counselor for several decades, I am often quick to recommend it. But not always. Counseling is not a substitute for something more fundamental, something quite within reach of Christians, especially, who have a grasp of the Christian meaning of love. The husband in this case was not innocent, a fact he readily admitted. But he had amended his ways, he had asked forgiveness, and was eager to move beyond their impasse to a renewed relationship. Since these were two intelligent, dedicated persons who loved each other and were not willing to give up their marriage, I agreed that forgiveness, not prolonged counseling, was the medicine needed to heal their relationship.

This is, after all, the essence of the gospel and of the church. The church of Christ is the community of the forgiven and forgiving. No Christian can boast of his or her right to membership. We come to the Lord in repentance; we are accepted by His forgiveness. We relate to one another, then, as fellow sinners who have received forgiveness. In the church, as elsewhere, "there is none righteous, no not one."

Tune Up

1. What is your most disturbing thought or question regarding forgiveness?

2. Why is the truth "there is none righteous, no not one" important to remember when we're struggling with forgiveness?

To the apostle Paul, this understanding of forgiveness is not just the theoretical or philosophical basis upon which the gospel rests ("we are saved by grace"), but it is the guiding principle in all human relationships in the church. He can be bold to ask Philemon to forgive his runaway slave Onesimus, in spite of the wrong Philemon has suffered, because of this principle. Read the entire letter closely. Then come back to this page and we'll look together at what it says about forgiveness.

We'll begin here:

Genuine forgiveness is rooted in faith and love.

"Love the Lord your God . . . and . . . your neighbor as yourself." Did Jesus say anything that is more quoted than this summary of the Law and the Prophets (Matthew 22:37)? I probably quote this one even more often than John 3:16, which is the best commentary on Matthew 22:37. Love, obviously, is a relationship word. Paul bases his appeal to Philemon equally on his "faith in the Lord Jesus" and his "love for all the saints." Confident that his friend is solidly grounded in these essentials, he hints at the appeal to come by disclosing his prayer for Philemon. "I pray that you may be active in sharing your faith, so that you will have a full understanding of every good thing we have in Christ." One of the best things we have in Christ, Philemon will learn, is the ability to forgive the unforgivable, to accept the unacceptable, and to do so not because of any formerly overlooked virtue in the offender, but because of the power of faith and love in the offended.

A French saying comes to our aid here: *Tout comprendre c'est tout pardonner,* "to understand is to forgive." But what is it that is being understood? To understand more fully the nature of the offense? But couldn't that equally force us to an even more resentful conclusion? To understand the deepest motives of the offender? Isn't the same heightened sense of injustice equally possible? The real issue at hand is our own offensiveness, isn't it? To understand our own sinful nature, our history of wrongs consciously or unconsciously inflicted on others (including the person we are currently so upset with), and the magnitude of God's grace in our own undeserving lives—isn't this what moves us to forgive?

Leslie Weatherhead put Jesus' teaching on this subject to the test during World War II in England. He chose to preach on Matthew 5:43, 44: "You have heard that it was said, 'Love your neighbor and hate your enemy.' But I tell you: Love your enemies and pray for those who persecute you." (You can't do this, can you, without a huge dose of forgiveness?)

Moving into his sermon, he told his bomb-blitzed London congregation that he wouldn't be surprised if his people asked him, "Do you expect us to love the Gestapo? Are you seriously asking us to love those who run concentration camps, persecute the Jews, lock up little children in filthy railway cars and send them to unknown destinations, tearing them away from their parents? Have you forgotten already the Nazi atrocities, the inhuman brutality. . . . We bomb them night after night as hard as we can. Do you suggest that on an eight-thousand-pound bomb we should tie a label, 'With love from Britain'? Surely it would be better if you forgot these words for the time being. At any rate, I'm not going to listen to such nonsense."[1]

Admitting the fairness of their sentiments—at a superficial level, we would have to add—he then powerfully challenged his people to love their enemy. Could we have done so? In the lifetime of my contemporaries, we have been taught to hate the German Nazis, the Italian Fascists, the Communist Russians, the Red Chinese, the militant Muslims, the American Negro, the Palestinians (or the Israelis, depending on our politics), and whoever else is the selected enemy of the moment, and often to hate them not for any particular offense but for their ideology or race or religion. What they have done or who they are is unforgivable.

How does that square, though, with Jesus' insistence that we must forgive—and only then shall we be forgiven (Luke 6:37)? Is it any wonder that before Paul makes his appeal he offers this reminder to Philemon? As a Christian, his life—thus his ethical stance and every moral decision—is grounded on his faith in Jesus Christ and his love of God and his neighbor, even his neighbor the runaway Onesimus.

Tune Up

1. How does understanding our own sinful nature help us forgive?

2. Who is your "selected enemy of the moment" as you read this book? Perhaps it's a terrorist or the leader of a seemingly diabolical nation—or your mother-in-law.

3. If you were able to pray for this "selected enemy" (Matthew 5:44), what would that prayer be?

Genuine forgiveness is voluntary, not forced.

"Therefore, although in Christ I could be bold and order you to do what you ought to do, yet I appeal to you on the basis of love."

If you have read through Paul's other letters, you are aware that he never doubts his authority as an apostle. Christ called him to his ministry and his high position in the church. When he must, he can bark orders and expect immediate obedience. He could, if he so chose, simply order Philemon to take back his erring slave. Undoubtedly Philemon would have obeyed. But that's all.

He would not have forgiven. His submission would have been begrudging, his later treatment of Onesimus probably harsh, and his mind unenlightened.

Obedience is expected here, of course. But not mere obedience to human or even ecclesiastical authority. It is obedience to the dictates of faith and love that Paul seeks for his friend. He hopes Philemon will do what he ought because that is what love, when it fully understands, does! Once love sees clearly, love forgives freely.

"Each time we forgive we absorb evil without passing it on," someone has said, "and then rise, like Christ, with healing in our wings."[2]

Bill and Judy Norris enjoyed a retirement ministry in England a few years ago. During their service there they met and marveled at the heart of Amy Jackson. They learned that Amy and her husband, Walter, patriotic Brits both, sent clothes and food to a German family in 1945, immediately after World War II ended but before all the bodies had been recovered. "How could you do that?" Judy asked Amy. "Didn't you have any sense of anger and hatred toward the nation that had hurt your people so much?" "I suppose we did. It's been so long ago. The main thing I remember is hearing that little children were hungry and cold."[3]

What Judy heard from Amy, we hear all the time from people who have caught the essence of forgiveness. It doesn't feel virtuous. It doesn't require superhuman strength or super-Christian spirituality. When your love and faith are genuine, your focus is not on your own feelings but on—well, on the hunger and cold that you can do something about, or on the open door and warm reception you can give your errant slave, or on the welcoming embrace and forgiving kiss you can plant on your offending spouse or other loved one.

Genuine forgiveness builds lasting relationships.

It isn't just temporary shelter Paul appeals for, or some experimental period to see whether Onesimus proves himself worthy of living once again in Philemon's home. Paul's goal instead is that Philemon "might have him back for good." Genuine forgiveness is not tentative and it is not conditional. "You have my forgiveness if or so long as . . ." is not forgiving; it is bargaining. You can't guarantee a permanent relationship at the negotiating table.

Donald Shriver, whose important book, *An Ethic for Enemies: Forgiveness in Politics,* expands on the theme we are exploring here, once said in a forum on the subject, "Forgiveness in politics has to do with how we manage our mutual relationships with the past without letting them manage us." To refuse to forgive is to be enslaved by the past. It is, quite literally, to be out of [our own] control, to be managed by someone or something else. Nothing liberates like forgiveness, in politics or anywhere else.

Two old political enemies, Thomas Jefferson and John Adams, were finally reconciled in their later years. Benjamin Rush helped bring these rivals together again, and the recorded correspondence of their last years is one of the treasures of American history. Rush called the men "the North and South Poles of the American Revolution." Writing to Mr. Adams, he paid the two patriots this glowing compliment: "Some talked, some wrote, and some fought to promote and establish it, but you and Mr. Jefferson thought for us all." In one of his letters, the voluble Adams wrote the less talkative Jefferson, "Never mind it, my dear Sir, if I write four letters to your one, your one is worth more than my four. . . . You and I ought not to die until we have explained ourselves to each other."[4]

And explain they did. They never came to complete accord on political issues. They did something far more important. They accepted the differences, they reaffirmed their admiration, they overcame their misunderstandings, they became reconciled. They forgave. After years of estrangement, their final years were warm and they died friends.

Genuine forgiveness recognizes the equality of those in gracious relationship.

Not as a slave but as a brother, Paul pleads, is how Onesimus is to be received. "So if you consider me a partner, welcome him as you would welcome me." You would not hesitate to offer me your hand; offer it to him. "If he has done you any wrong or owes you anything, charge it to me." Paul backs up this appeal by his offer to make any restitution on the slave's behalf. (He is putting his money where his mouth is!) Always the teacher, though, Paul then gently reminds Philemon once more that he, too, is a debtor ("I will pay it back—not to mention that you owe me your very self"). Without Paul, Philemon would not have met Christ; without the Lord, Philemon would be lost in unforgiven sin. Therefore . . .

One boast a Christian can never make: "In the eyes of God, I am your superior." No, in the eyes of God we are all equal sinners, all equally guilty. That we are in relation to God is due solely to His grace, not our worthiness. That we can have a relationship with one another is due to His grace and our own graciousness. We pass on the grace we have received. We feel neither superior nor inferior to another, hence we do not need to judge or rate (read berate) one another. We don't need to, but we do it anyway, don't we? We tend to write other people's job descriptions, mentally insist they meet all the demands in the description although we have never communicated this list to them, and then feel betrayed when the demands aren't met. It is not they who are at fault, but we. What right do we have to make such demands on others? Who made us their boss?

Tune Up

1. If you were Philemon, and Paul ordered you as an apostle to take Onesimus back, how would you feel?

2. Consider this phrase, "Each time we forgive we absorb evil without passing it on. And then rise, like Christ, with healing in our wings." In what ways is forgiveness healing, even when it isn't desired or asked for?

3. Why doesn't forgiveness feel virtuous or require super-human spirituality? (Check the Amy Jackson story for ideas.)

4. How might Paul's offer of restitution have made it easier for Philemon to accept back his slave Onesimus?

Abraham Lincoln, wise in so many ways, was wise in this one also: "On principle," he said, "I dislike an oath which requires a man to swear he has not done wrong. It rejects the Christian principle of forgiveness on terms of repentance. I think it enough if a man does not wrong hereafter."[5] (Would our hypercritical press and our hypocritical public allow such reasonableness in today's political arena?)

Grace, God's and ours. Allowing room for people's humanity, acknowledging our own sinfulness, giving thanks for our forgiveness with such sincerity that we gladly bring others into its embrace. On such graciousness lasting relationships are built.

A climactic moment at the end of the American Civil War dramatizes this equality. The confederate line was ready and the battle was about to be joined. General Sheridan's bugles sounded and all his brigades swung into line, ready to wipe out the slim Confederate lines. Then—"out from the Rebel lines came a lone rider, a young officer in a gray uniform," staff in hand with a white flag fluttering on the top of it. He asked to be taken to General Sheridan. The battlefield was quiet as he delivered his message of surrender. Historian Bruce Catton quotes two Union soldiers' reflections on that moment. "I remember how we sat there and pitied and sympathized with these courageous Southern men who had fought for four long and dreary years all so stubbornly, so bravely and so well, and now, whipped, beaten, completely used up, were fully at our mercy—it was pitiful, sad, hard, and seemed to us altogether too bad." A Pennsylvanian in the V Corps dodged past the skirmish line and strolled into the lines of the nearest Confederate regiment, and half a century after the war he recalled it with a glow: ". . . as soon as I got among these boys I felt and was treated as well as if I had been among our own boys, and a person would of thought we were of the same Army and had been Fighting under the Same Flag."6

The war was over. Reconciliation had begun between enemies who recognized they were far more alike than different. Where the differences were forgiven, peace was realized.

Grace expresses itself through genuine forgiveness.

By now the truth is obvious, isn't it? Grace is gracious. Grace forgives. Grace naturally expresses itself through forgiveness.

So Paul begins, "Grace to you and peace from God our Father and the Lord Jesus Christ." And he concludes, "The grace of the Lord Jesus Christ be with your spirit." A gracious Philemon—recipient of the grace of God, transmitter of the grace of God—will gladly forgive the erring Onesimus. The relationship will last.

Dave Stone reports that when Adolph Coors IV shared his testimony at the large Southeast Christian Church in Louisville he concluded, "If man's greatest need would have been for pleasure, then God would have sent an entertainer. If man's greatest need would have been for money, then He would have sent a financial consultant. If man's greatest need would have been information, He would have sent an educator.

"But God in His infinite wisdom knew that man's greatest need was forgiveness, and so He sent a Savior. Paul said, 'Therefore, there is now no condemnation for those who are in Christ Jesus'" (Romans 8:1).[7]

Mr. Coors has it right. So does Paul. We have been saved by grace. We simply pass it on.

It's the way of forgiveness.

Tune Up

1. Which of these expressions of grace is most interesting to you?
   - allowing room for people's humanity
   - acknowledging our own sinfulness
   - giving thanks for our forgiveness with such sincerity that we bring others into its embrace

2. In what way are you more like one of your personal "selected enemies of the moment" than different?

[1]Leslie D. Weatherhead, *The Significance of Silence.* New York: Abingdon Press, 1945.

[2]Cornelius Plantinga, Jr., "Rehearsing Forgiveness," *Christianity Today,* April 29, 1996.

[3]Judy Norris, "Amy Jackson: She Walks in Beauty," *The Lookout,* February 19, 1984.

[4]Page Smith, *The Shaping of America,* Volume 3. New York: McGraw-Hill, 1980.

[5]Quoted in Stephen L. Carter, *The Confirmation Mess.* New York: Basic Books, a division of HarperCollins, 1994, p. 31.

[6]Bruce Catton, *The Army of the Potomac: A Stillness at Appomattox.* Garden City: Doubleday, 1953.

[7]Dave Stone, *I'd Rather See a Sermon.* Joplin: College Press, 1996.

======= **CHAPTER 10** =======

THE WAY TO HEAVEN

Revelation 21:1-7; 21:22–22:7

While I was thinking through the subject of this chapter, the phone rang. It was my brother calling from Salem, Oregon, to tell me that fifteen minutes earlier our mother had died. The call was not a surprise. Mother was just four days short of her ninety-second birthday. She had been a victim of Alzheimer's Syndrome longer than anyone else I have ever known, having begun to slip into its depths seventeen years ago. For at least a decade she hadn't known anyone; for the last five years we were not able to sustain eye contact with her. She had left us a long time since. Only her body remained, somehow ingesting food and passing it through her digestive system. Alzheimer's is a dread disease.

We shed no tears as we talked, my brother and I. We had mourned our loss a long time ago. Reminding ourselves of the agreements we had drawn up for this day, ticking off the next steps, deciding who would call whom—these details filled the minutes of our conversation. The routines of burying the dead.

But the next several days were anything but routine. The body was not going to be buried in Tillamook, where she had lived since 1937, but rather in Yakima, Washington, in a plot reserved for her since the burial of her first husband who died in the automobile accident in 1935 that left her a widowed mother of a three-year-old. Since that tragic day she married twice more, gave birth to two more children, and never moved from our little Western Oregon county after settling there with her second husband in 1937. It seemed more than passing strange to conduct the quiet family grave-side service and consign her body to lie beside that young man killed so far in the past, my sister's father but a stranger to me.

Three days later the more formal memorial service was held in Salem. Once again I spoke, this time more at length. I uttered many of the customary words of comfort, read the usual Scriptures. My sister reflected briefly, my daughter and adoptive son provided the music. A few tears were shed but not many, because we were all relieved that this little lady had, at long last, laid aside her earthly garment, left her temporary dwelling and taken up more permanent lodging with her Father in Heaven.

In Heaven. The words came easily then, as they do now. As I prepared my remarks, I had to acknowledge the tremendous debt I owed my mother. She taught me faith. Dad didn't come from a deeply religious family; churchgoing was not habitual in his parents' home. It was Mother who insisted that our family would be in church. Dad agreed and, in fact, eventually became a leader in our congregation, probably at first to please her, then in time because he had embraced the faith and practiced it.

Like many other men, my faith took root from and was nurtured by a believing mother. And like many others, as I grew older I distanced myself from some of the particulars of her beliefs, struggling as she probably never had with some teachings I couldn't totally accept and some questions I couldn't easily dispel. What I became is probably quite different from what she envisioned, but the man and minister who is writing these pages has to admit that he would not—and could not—be doing so if it hadn't been for the faith of my mother.

Thanks to her, then, I can write this chapter about Heaven. One of the unshakable tenets of her steady faith was that life here is preparation for the real life to come over there, beyond the grave, in the presence of the Father, in the fellowship of all others (including her family and other loved ones). As her extended family gathered to say our final goodbyes, there was another reason (besides our relief that she had been released from Alzheimer's dread grip) for so few tears. There was general consensus that where she had gone was far better than where she had been. How could we weep when we considered her joy?

Tune Up

1. Consider your favorite song or hymn·about Heaven. What phrase do you like best in it?

2. How easy is it for you to accept that this tangible, very real life is only a preparation for a "real life" beyond the grave in the presence of God?

❏ easy   ❏ not so easy   ❏ very difficult

When the word comes that your loved one has died, questions concerning death and life after death move quickly from the theoretical to something very urgent, something demanding an answer. It isn't any surprise that the recently much-talked-about phenomenon called NDE, near death experience, has captured our attention. At first only whispered about by people who were afraid to tell their stories lest they be considered eccentric or even crazy, NDE is a hot topic that has found its way into headlines, magazines, and book-length studies. What should we call it? A peephole into a world beyond, as some have suggested? A merely physical recapitulation of the body's birth experience, with no overtones of the spiritual or eternal? Do some bodies actually die and come back to life? What exactly should we make of the talk shows and best-sellers and their tales of out of body experiences, most of which have a happy ending with a Being of Light granting forgiveness and blessing with peace and love?

Nearly one in five Americans claim at least once in their lifetimes to have been on the verge of dying, and one-third of these tell remarkable stories of entering that zone separating life and death. That means about 15 million people speak of an experience so real their lives are permanently changed. Could so many convinced people be wrong? When they "return" fully to their terrestrial life, they are much more serious than ever before about their spirituality. They no longer claim to believe in God; they know there is one. They believe they have proof.

Skeptics aren't so sure, though. They aren't convinced either about the existence of God or about whether these near death experiences actually point to any kind of life beyond the grave. They point out that the often cited phenomena common to these stories have now been reproduced experimentally. For example, by stimulating the brain's right temporal lobe, a person has a sensation of moving through a tunnel, at the end of which is a brilliant white light. This area above the right ear is responsible for perception; when prodded with mild electromagnetic fields, the desired effect is achieved. So did the near-death person really see the brilliant white light or was the brain somehow supercharged and merely simulating one?

A skeptical Carl Sagan offers another suggestion. He writes in *Broca's Brain*, "The only alternative, so far as I can see, is that every human being, without exception, has already had an experience like that of those travelers who return from the land of death: the sensation of flight; the emergence from darkness to light; an experience in which, at least sometimes, a heroic figure can be dimly perceived, bathed in radiance and glory. *There is only one common experience that matches this description. It is called birth."* He then identifies the feeling of bliss with the comfort of the womb and the oft-cited brilliant light with what a baby must experience at the end of the birth canal—and of course the doctor or midwife is the godlike figure.[1]

Betty Eadie, on the other hand, is a true believer. She claims she died, met Jesus, and came back to tell us about it. Her 1992 book, *Embraced by the Light,* was a best-seller, although its credibility has been seriously challenged. According to Eadie, Jesus was a being completely separate from the Father, He was careful not to offend her, and He wanted her not to regret her past. In addition, she says she learned human beings are not naturally sinful creatures. She consequently declared herself worthy to be with Jesus, even to embrace Him.

That's her story. Other testimonies differ. Some come back believing in God, others don't; some proclaim the mysteries of reincarnation, others don't; some speak of a Heaven-like atmosphere, others talk of darkness and torment.

I am introducing this near-death theme to get to a more serious point. Christian or non-Christian, believer or doubter, most of us find the issues of life after death and the possibility of Heaven fascinating. We grasp at any confirmation that the Scriptures are right about the future. It doesn't seem to bother us that people who have little to do with religion still have much to say about Heaven. We avidly read polls like the one that asked a thousand people, "Who will make it to Heaven?" Look at the results. These, the noted percentage of respondents assure us, will make it for sure:

Mother Teresa 79 percent
Oprah Winfrey, 66 percent
Michael Jordan, 65 percent
Colin Powell, 61 percent

Princess Diana, 60 percent
Bill Clinton, 52 percent
(Al Gore & Hillary Rodham Clinton got 55 percent)
Pat Robertson, 47 percent
Newt Gingrich, 40 percent
Dennis Rodman, 28 percent
O. J. Simpson, 19 percent

The poll results didn't reveal the criteria the respondents used for judging the eternal destination of these celebrities. Of course, that was the first standard: celebrity. What others? Sacrificial service? No, that would apply only to Mother Teresa. Athletic achievement obviously doesn't hurt. Political leadership? Not a sure thing. Certainly not political office or even religious leadership. And alleged murderers like O. J. Simpson or self-proclaimed bad boys like Dennis Rodman might want to hedge their bets.

One last statistic should be reported from this same poll. When asked whether they themselves would make it, 87 percent of the respondents assured the pollsters they would be there.

Do you think, in the final analysis, there is any difference between the calmness with which we commended our mother to God to take care of her forever in His dwelling place and the conviction of the near-death-experience survivors or the survey subjects who blithely place themselves in Heaven forever?

Or, to put my question somewhat differently, what right do I have to subject you to my thoughts on Heaven, I who have never had a NDE or been granted like the apostle Paul a glimpse of the third Heaven (2 Corinthians 12)? I'll admit that I have very little to say on the subject. In the literal meaning of the word, I have to plead a case of *agnosticism* —that is, I don't know (*a*=not; *gnosis*=known). In one sense I am very much like the apostle Paul, who wrote in 1 Corinthians 13:12, "Now we see but a poor reflection as in a mirror; then we shall see face to face. Now I know in part; then I shall know fully, even as I am fully known." Not until

I see "face to face" will I be able to write with any authority on this subject. I've only looked from the bottom up; I know only what the earthbound can know.

But that doesn't mean that earthlings like you and me are clueless. Some of the best tips, as a matter of fact, are found in the last book of the Bible, the Revelation. Let's look at a couple of favorite Scriptures on the subject, in the last two chapters of the Bible.

What we shall see isn't what we have seen.

> Then I saw a new heaven and a new earth, for the first heaven and the first earth had passed away, and there was no longer any sea. I saw the Holy City, the new Jerusalem, coming down out of heaven from God, prepared as a bride beautifully dressed for her husband. And I heard a loud voice from the throne saying, "Now the dwelling of God is with men, and he will live with them. They will be his people, and God himself will be with them and be their God. He will wipe every tear from their eyes. There will be no more death or mourning or crying or pain, for the old order of things has passed away."
>
> He who was seated on the throne said, "I am making everything new!" Then he said, "Write this down, for these words are trustworthy and true."
>
> Revelation 21:1-5

The words are familiar. As I read them for Mother's service, several people nodded in recognition. They knew the promise. They liked it.

What we like is the way one little word dominates the paragraph: new. We've had enough of the old. It hasn't been kind to us. We long for a new Heaven and a new earth, a new Jerusalem, a new kind of relationship with God (a bride beautifully dressed for her husband), one in which we can experience a new closeness with God. What could be more reassuring than to hear the voice of God saying, "I am making everything new"?

We gathered around my sister's picture albums and marveled at the beauty of Mother as a young bride, fashionably
dressed and coiffured, skin unblemished and smooth, eyes
laughing and, truth to tell, a little coy. We didn't say so, but I
suspect others were thinking as I was about the stark contrast between her young beauty and the ravaged body of her
last years, a cruel caricature of her former radiance. There
was nothing I wanted more for her than to be, once again, a
bride, a personal expression of the bride of Christ Paul
writes of in Ephesians and that John envisions here in Revelation. We wanted our mother to be new.

Of course, this language is poetic. It suggests but does not
exhaust the possibilities. We can't limit God's creative imagination to the outer boundaries of our own. What we shall see
isn't what we have seen here on this finite, temporary planet
inhabited by transients who are only tenting here on their way
to something better. We don't know what the future holds, as
the song goes, but we do know "we ain't seen nothing yet."

Tune Up

1. Underline the promises found in Revelation 21:1-8.

2. How does the last phrase of Revelation 21:5 compare
with all the conjecture on near death experiences?

We shall be able to see what is to be seen.

John's revelatory vision is most astonishing in what it takes for granted—what we assume without thinking: when we get to Heaven, we shall be able to see what is to be seen.

I've already confessed that there's much about Heaven I don't know. One reality seems to come through in all the Bible's allusions to it, though, and through the teaching of the great writers of the faith, and that is that though our bodies return to dust, our consciousness never dies. We don't somehow merge into the great Oversoul, a popular doctrine earlier in American history. We don't disappear into a great abyss. Something about us remains, remains recognizable, and has the ability to see and know.

The apostle Paul says we get spiritual bodies, incorruptible, imperishable, glorious, and powerful (1 Corinthians 15). The book of Revelation shows these spiritualized saved ones surrounding the throne of God, praising and glorying in their new life, thoroughly enjoying what they can see and experience.

Paul was so convinced of the good life on the other side of the grave that, when wondering whether he would get out of prison alive or not he could tell his friends it didn't really matter to him whether he did or didn't: "I am torn between the two: I desire to depart and be with Christ, which is better by far; but it is more necessary for you that I remain in the body" (Philippians 1:23, 24). For his friends' sake he could be pleased to stay alive; for his own, he would be just as happy to get his death over with so he could enjoy a new life, seeing what is to be seen, being what he will become.

The Communion of God and His people is consummated.

No temple in Heaven, and neither sun nor moon nor lamp.
No gates to shut at night, and no night.
No longer will there be any curse.

"The throne of God and of the Lamb will be in the city, and his servants will serve him. They will see his face, and his name will be on their foreheads" (Revelation 22:3, 4). And in the presence of God, all other light is superfluous.

Here we seek God. There He is found.

Here we cry in the night and curse the darkness. There all is day and nothing deserves the curse.

Here we are lonely and at odds; there we are with the One who wants us and the ones who want Him and us.

Here we are nobody. There we are His and are known by His name on our brows.

Tune Up

1. Based on the 1 Corinthians 15 description of our new bodies, how will your new body be different from the way it is now on earth?

2. What does it appear that the saved ones will do, and apparently enjoy doing?

3. What would have to be true of someone in order for him or her not to care whether he or she lived or died, to think that death is much better (as Paul said in Philippians 1:23, 24)?

4. Underline the phrases in the reading and Scripture above that has the most appeal for you.

I didn't know the redheaded, freckle-faced, twelve-year-old boy I learned about from a South African pastor I met when visiting his country in 1997. Charles Gordon tells of a very sick charwoman in London whose friends' generosity made it possible for her to go to the hospital. Her confinement was what she needed, and her healing began. While still convalescing there, she became acquainted with other patients, among them this youngster. His room was across the hall. She talked with him daily. One morning a commotion in the hall woke her. Then into her own room came the boy's mother. "The doctors say Johnny has about ten minutes to live," she said. "Won't you say something to him?"

She went immediately, internally struggling with the difficult assignment. Words were not her forte. She sat down beside him, took his hand, and quietly but directly said, "Listen, John. God made you. God loves you. God sent His Son

to save you. God wants you to come home to live with Him."
He had just enough strength left to turn his eyes toward her
and whisper, "Say it again." "God made you," she repeated.
"God loves you. God sent His Son to save you. God wants
you to come home to live with Him." He took her words in.
Then calmly he spoke again, "Tell God, 'Thank you.'"[2]

What better words can you say, when you come to the end
of the way?

The pain of earth-life is abolished.

"There will be no more death or mourning or crying or
pain, for the old order of things has passed away."

And nothing impure will pollute.

And rivalries will cease.

And national boundaries will disappear.

And war will not even be remembered.

And tears shall cease.

The journey is over.

We will have come home.

The telephone rang twice as I was writing this chapter. I
have already written about the call from my brother saying
that our mother was gone. The second was from my administrative assistant. Two of our church members had died in
the last twenty-four hours, she said. Arlene was in her late
70s, John 84. Both had surpassed their biblical three-score
and ten; both had lived their years in the Lord. Neither
feared death, and when they died, each left behind a spouse
who spoke peacefully of personal loss but at the same time
of their loved one's gain. John had fretted about leaving
Thelma with no one to take care of her, but by the time I
talked with Thelma she had already decided she would sell
their home of thirty years and move into the Christian retirement center in our city. She thought her separation from
John would be brief. Arlene, who had suffered with severe

asthma and other debilitating illnesses, had been preparing for her homecoming for years. Her husband, Bob, was at peace, because she was.

As far as their spouses were concerned, they could rejoice. The journey of their loved ones was over. They had known the way to Heaven.

So did my mother. So I, too, rejoice.

Tune Up

1. Consider the phrases under the heading: The pain of earth-life is abolished. What gifts (such as peace) would these realities mean for people such as:
   • CEOs of companies being hammered by bigger companies?
   • war veterans with painful memories?
   • refugees who flee when a new boundary line forces them from their home?

3. Name other individuals or groups who will benefit from conditions in the new Heaven.

4. Name an elderly person in your church who is mature in Christ. If you were to ask him or her about his or her hope of Heaven, what would your opening question be?

[1]Quoted in *Evangelical Newsletter,* April 6, 1979.

[2]Charles Gordon, *Vitamins for Your Soul.* Durban North, South Africa: Good Shepherd Press.